Private Sector Housing and Health

This book is an evaluation of the effectiveness of housing enforcement and tenant protection in England's private rented sector using policy analysis to evaluate regulatory provisions and local authority guidance to identify the advantages and limitations of existing policies. From the environmental health practitioner perspective, the targeted health problem is occupiers privately renting from negligent or criminal landlords who are subsequently exposed to hazardous conditions arising from disrepair.

Paul Oatt's analysis looks at the powers local authorities have to address retaliatory eviction when enforcing against housing disrepair and digs deeper into their duties to prevent homelessness and powers to protect tenants from illegal eviction. He then explores the potential for tenants to take private action against landlords over failures to address disrepair, before finally discussing proposals put forward by the government to abolish retaliatory evictions and improve security of tenure with changes to contractual arrangements between landlords and tenants, based on successive stakeholder consultations. The policy analysis looks at these aspects to define the overall effectiveness of housing strategies and their implementation, examining causality, plausibility and intervention logic as well as the unintended effects on the population. Equitability is examined to see where policy effects create inequalities as well as the costs, feasibility and acceptability of policies from landlords' and tenants' perspectives.

The book will be of relevance to professionals interested in housing and health, as well as students at universities that teach courses in environmental health, public health, and housing studies.

Paul Oatt is Chartered Environmental Health Practitioner with over 20 years' experience in local government housing regulation up to the management level. He qualified with a BSc (Hons) in Environmental Health from Middlesex University and an MSc in Public Health from the London School of Hygiene and Tropical Medicine. Paul is currently a doctoral student at Middlesex University and works part-time as a course trainer and lecturer in the subjects of environmental health and public health. Also, he tutors at the University of Greenwich. He is the author of *Selective Licensing: The Basis for a Collaborative Approach to Addressing Health Inequalities* (2019).

Routledge Focus on Environmental Health

Series Editor: Stephen Battersby, MBE PhD, FCIEH, FRSPH

For more information about this series, please visit: https://www.routledge.com

Private Sector Housing and Health

Evaluating the Effectiveness
of Regulation Intended to Protect
the Health of Tenants

Paul Oatt

Routledge
Taylor & Francis Group

LONDON AND NEW YORK

Chartered Institute of
Environmental Health

First published 2025
by Routledge
4 Park Square, Milton Park, Abingdon, Oxon OX14 4RN

and by Routledge
605 Third Avenue, New York, NY 10158

Routledge is an imprint of the Taylor & Francis Group, an informa business

British Library Cataloguing-in-Publication Data
A catalogue record for this book is available from the British Library

ISBN: 978-1-032-69305-7 (hbk)
ISBN: 978-1-032-70505-7 (pbk)
ISBN: 978-1-032-70507-1 (ebk)

DOI: 10.1201/9781032705071

Typeset in Times New Roman
by Apex CoVantage, LLC

Contents

Acknowledgements

I would like to thank everyone who has supported me in the research and the making of this book. It might seem a strange thing to say but the development of this publication came about almost by accident. My doctoral research is in housing enforcement and enforcement officer practices. In analysing and filtering out relevant papers for those purposes, it became apparent to me that there is a large area of research around issues with landlords and tenants that is of immense importance and could potentially have been overlooked.

Both arms of my research examine the advantages and limitations of regulatory provisions but from different perspectives. My primary doctoral research is examining this from the perspective of a housing enforcer in the current regulatory landscape. This book examines reformation of policies towards the private rented sector intended to protect tenants' rights, reduce adverse health effects and empower them to challenge poor landlord practices as well as provide landlords with more control over property management. The focus here is different because it uses research on what is known about the effectiveness and unintended effects and inequalities prevalent within existing systems from the perspectives of tenants and landlords and the feasibility of reformation in the current housing market where there is a shortage of affordable rental accommodation, a local authority duty to house, a high prevalence of retaliatory evictions, unlawful harassment and forced removal and the ensuing negative health effects.

I owe an immense debt of gratitude to my supervisors Doctor Jill Stewart and Doctor Ruth Plume at Middlesex University for encouraging me to seek out a separate outlet in which to develop and publish these findings that would otherwise have been discarded in pursuit of my primary research.

Thanks also to Doctor Stephen Battersby and Ed Needle at Routledge, Taylor and Francis, for their encouragement and invaluable guidance through the publication process. My thanks also to the L'Institut national de santé publique du Québec, for permission to reproduce the diagram of the Morestin's framework of relationships between the six analytical dimensions.

Lastly, I would like to thank my wife, Jenny, and my daughter, Phoenix, for all their support and without whom this would not have been possible.

Abbreviations

ACORN	Association of Community Organizations for Reform Now
APPG PRS	All Party Parliamentary Group for the Private Rented Sector
AST	Assured Shorthold Tenancy
ATRO	Association of Tenancy Relations Officers
BAME	Black, Asian, Minority Ethnic
CIEH	Chartered Institute of Environmental Health
CLGC	Communities and Local Government Committee
CLGSC	Communities and Local Government Select Committee
DCLG	Department for Communities and Local Government
DLUHC	Department for Levelling Up, Housing and Communities
EHS	English Housing Survey
HCCPA	House of Commons Committee of Public Accounts
H-CLIC	Homelessness Case Level Information Collection
HHSRS	Housing Health and Safety Rating System
HMO	House in Multiple Occupation
LARG	Large Agents Representation Group
LASPO	Legal Aid, Sentencing and Punishment of Offenders Act 2012
LBW	Low Birth Weight
LGA	Local Government Association
MHCLG	Ministry of Housing, Communities and Local Government
NAO	National Audit Office
NRLA	National Residential Landlords Association
OBR	Office for Budget Responsibility
ODPM	Office of the Deputy Prime Minister
ONS	Office of National Statistics
PACE	Police and Criminal Evidence Act 1984

PCM	Per Calendar Month
PTB	Pre-term Birth
TDS	Tenancy Deposit Scheme
VLBW	Very Low Birth Weight
VOA	Valuation Office Agency

Series Preface

This is the fifteenth publication in the series, with more in the pipeline.

The aim of the series remains as ever; to explore environmental health topics traditional or new and raise sometimes contentious issues in more detail than might be found in the usual environmental health texts. It is also a means whereby environmental health issues can be discussed with a wider audience in mind.

This series is an important part of the professional landscape, as is apparent from the titles published so far. Environmental health practitioners bring their expertise to a range of situations and are deployed differently but not always to the best effect so far as public health is concerned. All too often politicians both at the national and local levels are unaware of what is environmental health, and what practitioners do or how they work. It is common that practitioners have a 'low profile' or are taken for granted. It is hoped that this series will be used as a means of highlighting the work of environmental health practitioners.

We want to encourage readers and practitioners, particularly those who might not have had work published previously, to submit proposals as we hope to be responsive to the needs of environmental and public health practitioners. I am particularly keen that this series is seen as an opportunity for first-time authors and as ever would urge students (whether at first- or second-degree level) to consider this an avenue for publishing findings from their research. Why for example should the hard work that has gone into a dissertation or thesis lie unread on a library shelf? We can provide advice on turning a thesis into a book. Equally this series can be a way of extending a presentation, paper or training materials, so that these can reach a wider audience.

The series provides a route for practitioners to improve the profile of the profession as well as provide a source of information. It has the advantage of having a relatively quick turn around from submission of the manuscript to publication and can be more up to date and immediate than a standard textbook or reference work.

It seems that EHPs have perhaps not been good at telling others about their work and contribution to public health. To be considered a genuine profession and to develop professionally EHPs on the front line need to "get published", writing up their work of protecting public health. This series is a route for analysing actions and reporting on what worked in practice, what was successful what wasn't and why. This can provide useful insights for others working in the field and also highlight policy issues of relevance to environmental health.

Contributing to this series should not be seen merely as an exercise in gathering CPD hours but a useful method of reflection and an aid to career development, something that anyone who considers themselves a professional should do. I am pleased to be working with Routledge to provide this opportunity for practitioners.

As has been made clear it is not intended that this series takes a wholly "technical" approach but provides an opportunity to consider areas of practice in a different way, for example looking at the social and political aspects of environmental health in addition to a more discursive approach on specialist areas.

Our hope remains that this is a dynamic series, providing a forum for new ideas and debate on environmental health topics. If readers have any ideas for titles in the series, please do not be afraid to submit them to me as series editor via the e-mail addresses below.

"Environmental health" can be taken to mean different things in different countries around the World and so we welcome suggestions from a range of professions doing "environmental health" work or policy development. EHPs may be a key part of the public health workforce wherever they practise, but there also many other practitioners working to safeguard public and environmental health. It is hoped that this series will enable a wider range of practitioners and others with a professional interest to access information and also to write about issues relevant to them.

Forthcoming monographs are likely to cover such topics as air pollution and monitoring private water supplies. We are in contact with colleagues around the world encouraging them to submit proposals. That does not mean we have no need of further suggestions, quite the contrary, so I hope readers with ideas for a monograph will get in touch via Ed.Needle@tandf.co.uk or Martha.Luke@tandf.co.uk

Stephen Battersby MBE PhD, FCIEH, FRSPH
Series Editor

1 Introduction

Unfortunately, UK housing regulation is not neatly contained within an all-encapsulating policy but divided amongst various statutory instruments (National Audit Office (NAO), 2021). The now defunct Renters (Reform) Bill whose enactment in Parliament was halted by the general election, was an attempt to address long-standing issues in landlords and tenant law (Cobbold, 2024). Whilst Assured Shorthold Tenancies (ASTs) were intended to provide security of tenure, simultaneously a provision under Section 21 of the Housing Act 1988 allows landlords to carry out 'no-fault evictions' upon tenants without giving any reason (Wilson and Cromarty, 2023). Should tenants remain in the property upon the expiry of a Section 21 notice, eviction procedures are accelerated when landlords apply to the courts for possession. The courts send a notice of issue to both parties, giving the tenant 14 days to file a defence, which is problematic because tenants cannot easily raise objections against eviction if the landlord's reason is unknown to them (Phillips, 2022).

Being able to evict tenants outside of the fixed period of the tenancy without justification promotes insecurity of tenure (Gousy, 2014; Lonegrass, 2015; Reeve-Lewis et al., 2022). The StepChange Debt Charity provided written evidence to the House of Commons Committee of Public Accounts (HCCPA) (2022a) of a power imbalance inherent within housing eviction processes creating difficulties for financially vulnerable tenants to enforce their rights. In terms of policy implementation, security of tenure through ASTs on one hand and 'no-fault evictions' on the other seem incompatible. The Renters (Reform) Bill proposed to abolish Section 21 evictions, landlords seeking possession would have to specify grounds for eviction using Section 8 of the Housing Act 1988 with numerous amendments under Schedule 2 of the act (The Department of Levelling up, Housing and Communities (DLUHC), 2023a, 2023b; Wilson and Cromarty, 2023).

DOI: 10.1201/9781032705071-1

Housing legislation is splintered into grounds that landlords rely upon for eviction and gaining possession of their properties under the Housing Act 1988. Local authority regulatory powers for these properties are found within the Housing Act 2004. The Homes (Fitness for Human Habitation) Act 2018 provides tenants with a means to take legal action against landlords. The Protection from Eviction Act 1977 protects tenants from illegal eviction or harassment whilst the Deregulation Act 2015 protects tenants from retaliatory evictions.

Owing to this fragmentation of policies, the housing policy analysis carried out in this work required a policy framework that lends itself to the examination and contextualisation of variable policy and regulatory sources as well as supporting data. Morestin's framework for analysing public policies (Morestin, 2012) facilitates the use of multiple sources in policy examination through the lens of public health to explore the feasibility of a proposed policy and the effectiveness of policies that oversee landlord and tenant interactions, some of which are health-based, or where public health has formed part of the decision-making process. The analysis also looks at research commissioned by the central government, its findings and how this has influenced and shaped government policy.

The knowledge base on housing and health is still small (Egan et al., 2022). Most research into health impacts of housing instability and insecurity of tenure in the private rented sector were carried out in overseas studies. Coley et al. (2013) observed these studies often lack a multi-dimensional focus concentrating on associations between one exposure at a time failing to acknowledge that exposures such as housing quality, stability, affordability, ownership and subsidy receipt status do not occur in isolation. They also noted in studies examining associations between poor housing conditions and children's wellbeing, a parent's access to good steady well-paid employment and affordable good-quality housing allows the creation of family stability with the derived benefit of positively influencing children's cognitive, emotional and behavioural outcomes.

The DLUHC (2023c) impact assessment of the Renters (Reform) Bill draws upon overseas longitudinal studies on residential mobility in childhood demonstrating that disrupting children's education through moves associated with insecurity of tenure leads to children's poor attainment in literacy and maths, increasing the likelihood of dropping out of high school, poor employment prospects and low income, as opposed to children who remain in the same schools with less residential mobility, who graduate and go on to earn within higher-income brackets (Coley and Kull, 2016; Tønnessen et al., 2016).

In the UK, many studies on housing and health have explored poor housing conditions and areas of deprivation, socio-economic disadvantages and poor health outcomes for tenants (Marmot, 2010; Pevalin et al., 2008; Thomson et al., 2013). But much of the research on the impacts of forced eviction whether legal or illegal, and tenure insecurity were carried out overseas, notably in America. For this reason, like the DLUHC, it is necessary for the purposes of this study to examine the findings of these studies to appreciate the scale of the problem, subsequent health impacts and reasons for many of the underlying causes leading to eviction and its consequences. This study draws upon widespread material to illustrate with supporting data the many ways in which eviction, however it is carried out, impacts health and social inequalities.

The analysis of the effects and implementation of the chosen policy is carried out across six dimensions: effectiveness, unintended effects, equity, cost, feasibility and acceptability.

The policy analysis uses the dimensions shown under effects in Figure 1.1 beginning with effectiveness to determine success through the outcomes and whether they fulfil the policies intended use to prevent or remedy. For many long-term policies, it is recognised that outcomes take a long time to emerge. Often causality and temporality of association are unclear, for this reason, Morestin's framework also assesses effects at the intermediate level.

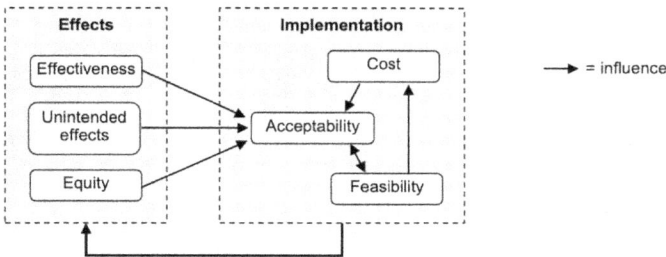

Figure 1.1 Relationships between the six analytical dimensions.
Source: (Morestin, 2012)

The UK housing market is no different to many other developed countries currently facing a housing crisis, unable to meet the demand for affordable quality housing, adversely impacting security of tenure for vulnerable adults (Hafford-Letchfield et al., 2019). During the past two decades, England's private rented sector almost doubled in size (DLUHC, 2022; Ministry of Housing, Communities and Local Government (MHCLG), 2020). Growth is attributed to various market forces, including the creation of ASTs as well as selling off social housing stock during the late 1990s and early 2000s (Pawson et al., 2009) and the introduction of buy-to-let mortgages (Miller, 2010).

The Renters (Reform) Bill was an attempt to ensure equitability within the private rented sector through reformation. This was envisioned to be achieved not just through the abolition of Section 21 of the Housing Act 1988 and replacement with amendments to other eviction grounds but also by introducing a new private rented property portal, Ombudsman, and redress scheme to provide tenants security of tenure within safer, better-maintained properties that can be treated as their own home. Where this is not the case, the bills' purpose was to empower tenants to use redress to 'challenge poor practice' and effectively resolve issues for both landlords and tenants. Simultaneously, the government wished to ensure landlords are provided with sufficient information on what is expected of them to achieve compliance and what avenues are available to them for repossession when required (All Party Parliamentary Group for the Private Rented Sector, APPG-PRS), 2023; DLUHC, 2023c). The bill contained additional enforcement tools for local authorities to enforce financial penalties or prosecution for breaches of these new regulations and were intended to assist them with regulating poor practices (DLUHC, 2023c; Wilson and Cromarty, 2023).

This study highlights the potential pitfalls by assessing effectiveness and health to consider solutions. The analytical framework used enabled the incorporation of data from wide-ranging sources to contribute to the existing body of literature and broaden the scope. The analysis was carried out through the lens of public health to better inform policy makers and identify weaknesses and solutions with an evidence-informed approach. Ultimately, it is hoped the findings will go some way towards ensuring that eviction rates whether legal, informal or unlawful reduce through positively influencing the associated social determinants of health in this sector.

References

APPG for the Private Rented Sector. (2023, December). *Ensuring Rental Reform Works for Tenants and Landlords. A Vision for the Private Rented Sector of the Future*. Propertymark. Available from: https://www.propertymark.co.uk/static/fe6fd918-c274-405f-813539a518191797/Ensuring-Rental-Reform-Works-for-Tenants-and-Landlords.pdf

Cobbold, N. (2024 May 31). Renters (Reform) Bill dead. Reapit. Available at; https://www.reapit.com/content-hub/renters-reform-bill-dead

Coley, R.L. and Kull, M. (2016). 'Cumulative, Timing-Specific, and Interactive Models of Residential Mobility and Children's Cognitive and Psychosocial Skills', *Child Development*, 87(4), pp. 1204–1220.

Coley, R.L., Leventhal, T., Lynch, A.D. and Kull, M. (2013, September). *Poor Quality Housing is Tied to Children's Emotional and Behavioral Problems. Policy Research Brief*. Chicago: MacArthur Foundation.

Department for Levelling Up, Housing and Communities. (2022, December). *English Housing Survey Headline Report 2021–22*. London: DLUHC.

Department for Levelling Up, Housing and Communities. (2023a, May 17). Renters (Reform) Bill 308-2022-23 (as Introduced). UK Parliament. Parliamentary Bills. [online]. Available from: https://publications.parliament.uk/pa/bills/cbill/58-03/0308/220308.pdf

Department for Levelling Up, Housing and Communities. (2023b, May 17). 'Guide to the Renters (Reform) Bill', *GOV.UK*. [online]. Available from: https://www.gov.uk/guidance/guide-to-the-renters-reform-bill

Department for Levelling Up, Housing and Communities. (2023c, May 12). *Renters (Reform) Bill Impact Assessment: DLUHC 2564*. London: House of Commons.

Deregulation Act 2015 c.20. Available from: https://www.legislation.gov.uk/ukpga/2015/20/contents/enacted

Egan, M., Rinaldi, C., Petersen, J., Seguin, M. and Marks, D. (2022). 'Embedding Research on Public Health and Housing into Practice', in Stewart, J. and Moffatt, R. (Eds), *Regulating the Privately Rented Housing Sector*. Abingdon, Oxon: Routledge, pp. 97–105.

Gousy, H. (2014). *Safe and Decent Homes: Solutions for a Better Private Rented Sector*. London: Shelter.

Hafford-Letchfield, T., Gleeson, H. and Mohammed, R. (2019). 'Vulnerable Adults in the Privately Rented Sector in England: A Snapshot of Current Practice Issues', *Practice (Birmingham, England)*, 31(2), pp. 97–115.

Homes (Fitness for Human Habitation) Act 2018 c.34. Available from: https://www.legislation.gov.uk/ukpga/2018/34/enacted (accessed 22 October 2023).

House of Commons Committee of Public Accounts. (2022a, January). Written Evidence Submitted by StepChange Debt Charity. PRP0005.

Housing Act 1988 c.50. Available from: https://www.legislation.gov. uk/ukpga/1988/50/contents

Housing Act 2004 c.34. Available from: https://www.legislation.gov. uk/ukpga/2004/34/contents

Lonegrass, M.T. (2015). 'Eliminating Landlord Retaliation in England and Wales – Lessons from the United States', *Louisiana Law Review*, 75(4), pp. 1071–1123.

Marmot, M. (2010). *Fair Society, Healthy Lives: The Marmot Review: Strategic Review of Health Inequalities in England Post 2010*. London: University College London.

Miller, L. (2010, November 1). *Private Rented Extra Care: A New Market? Factsheet 32. Housing LIN Housing Learning & Improvement Network*. London: DoH, NAO.

Ministry of Housing, Communities and Local Government. (2020). *English Housing Survey: Headline Report 2019–2020*. London: MHCLG.

Morestin, F. (2012, September). *A Framework for Analyzing Public Policies: Practical Guide*. National Collaborating Centre for Healthy Public Policy. [online]. Available from: http://www.ncchpp. ca/docs/Guide_framework_analyzing_policies_En.pdf

National Audit Office. (2021, December 10). *Regulation of Private Renting: HC 863*. London: Department for Levelling Up, Housing & Communities.

Pawson, H., Davidson, E., Morgan, J., Smith, R. and Edwards, R. (2009, February 27). *The Impacts of Housing Stock Transfers in Urban Britain*. Chartered Institute of Housing: Joseph Rowntree Foundation.

Pevalin, D.J., Taylor, M.P. and Todd, J. (2008). 'The Dynamics of Unhealthy Housing in the UK: A Panel Data Analysis', *Housing Studies*, 23(5), pp. 679–695.

Phillips, A. (2022, June 9). *Accelerated Possession Procedure vs Standard Possession Procedure*. Holmes and Hills Solicitors. [online]. Available from: https://www.holmes-hills.co.uk/news/2022/june/ accelerated-possession-procedure-vs-standard-possession-procedure/

Protection from Eviction Act 1977 c.43. Available from: https://www. legislation.gov.uk/ukpga/1977/43

Reeve-Lewis, B., Bolton, J.L. and Rugg, J. (2022, May). *Offences Under the Protection from Eviction Act 1977 in England and Wales: A Report from Safer Renting*. London: Safer Renting. Cambridge House.

Renters (Reform) Bill. (2023, December 7). *Department for Levelling Up, Housing and Communities*. London: House of Commons.

Thomson, H., Thomas, S., Sellstrom, E. and Petticrew, M. (2013). 'Cochrane Public Health Group. Housing Improvements for Health and Associated Socioeconomic Outcomes', in *Cochrane Database of Systematic Reviews.* [online]. Available from: https://www.cochranelibrary.com/cdsr/doi/10.1002/14651858.CD008657.pub2/epdf/full

Tønnessen, M., Telle, K. and Syse, A. (2016). 'Childhood Residential Mobility and Long-Term Outcomes', *Acta Sociologica,* 59(2), pp. 113–129.

Wilson, W. and Cromarty, H. (2023, October 21). *Research Briefing: Renters (Reform) Bill 2022-23: CBP08756.* London: House of Commons Library.

2 Eviction and Its Health Effects

Before moving onto the policy analysis covered in the next chapters, this section examines the known socioeconomic stressors and physical and mental health outcomes affecting tenants privately renting who live under the threat of potential eviction or endured displacement either lawfully or illegally. The chapter draws upon UK and overseas studies. It is recognised that other health care systems are administered using completely different guidelines and regulations. UK healthcare is free at the point of service funded through progressive taxation through national insurance contributions. In America, employee's healthcare is funded through private company insurance through monthly deductibles and co-payments. Public insurance is via Medicaid for those qualifying on low incomes (DeGrazia Jr et al., 2023; Jacob, 2023; Ozawa, 2011).

Globally, studies on housing instability amongst tenants and their children strongly link to poor mental health outcomes (Desmond and Kimbro, 2015; Hatch and Yun, 2021; Hoke and Boen, 2021; Petersen et al., 2022). Arguably forcible eviction is a social determinant of health creating a 'unique stressor' where impacts of associated socioeconomic risk factors increase upon population health (Hoke and Boen, 2021; Tunstall et al., 2010; Zewde et al., 2019).

In households experiencing multiple moves within short periods, strong associations were found with poor school performance amongst 2,400 American children, teens and young adult pupils with lower reading and maths skills from deprived areas within Boston, Chicago and San Antonio (Coley et al., 2013). Priced out of urban rental markets, many low-income households moved into older properties within suburban areas lured by cheaper rents, better schools and economic prospects (Desmond, 2018; Hazekamp et al., 2021; Hepburn et al., 2020).

DOI: 10.1201/9781032705071-2

Filing for eviction creates searchable public documents that present difficulties for American tenants trying to relocate. Filing is often used to threaten tenants to elicit repayment of arrears, or prompt voluntary departure thus avoiding court proceedings (Biederman et al., 2022; Hazekamp et al., 2021; Lonegrass, 2015; Moran-McCabe and Burris, 2021; Zewde et al., 2019). Many families surveyed about previous evictions only confirmed evictions verifiable under-documented court orders; informal evictions are often discounted and are exacerbating an eviction crisis across America where the true frequency of evictions is greatly underestimated (Desmond, 2016; Hatch and Yun, 2021; Hazekamp et al., 2021).

Health effects from American evictees aged between 18 and 34 were measured using self-reported mental health disorders such as depression, anxiety and panic disorders. Associations were found between evictions and health with stronger health impacts in the short term (12 months post-eviction). Impacts lessened over seven to eight years post-eviction but remained prevalent amongst women and non-White research participants illustrating relationships between eviction and health are disproportionate amongst demographic groups (Acharya et al., 2022; Hatch and Yun, 2021).

Knowing that eviction is pending creates a psychosocial stressor (Hoke and Boen, 2021; Vasquez-Vera et al., 2017). UK-based debt counselling charity StepChange reported that 54,000 private rented sector tenants, half with physical or mental health vulnerabilities, required support with rental arrears in 2021. Insecurity of tenure reportedly affected the health of half of these tenants, whilst almost a third reported poor-quality housing affecting either their own health or their family's health. Almost two-thirds said debt problems had meant a reduction in the quality of housing. Twenty-nine per cent of residents were exposed to hazards through lack of insulation, water leaks, damp and condensation. Thirty-eight per cent of these private rented sector tenants spent more on energy bills (HCCPA, 2022). Shelter (2021) reported that 26% of UK private rented sector tenants also exposed to damp and mould struggle to heat their homes. Nineteen per cent of tenants experiencing these issues or who feared possible eviction considered these problems harmful to their health. The inability to adequately heat a home can result in disease or exacerbate existing conditions (Rudge and Gilchrist, 2005; Sawyer et al., 2022).

A London housing market study examined primary impacts of selective licensing schemes on mental health outcomes for private rented sector tenants and neighbourhood anti-social behaviour (Petersen et al., 2022). Selective licensing allows local authorities to designate poor housing areas for licensing requiring private landlords to maintain properties to a basic set of licence conditions, including providing tenants written agreements, ensuring properties are not overcrowded and maintenance of gas, electrical and fire safety (Oatt, 2019). Petersen et al. (2022) used population survey data and examined licensing schemes in London designated between 2012 and 2018 to assess the impact on self-reported wellbeing and mental health, as well as neighbourhood antisocial behaviour and frequent changes in tenure. They examined 921 intervention lower super output areas with approximately three-to-one comparison groups (3,684 in total) comparing changes in outcome over time examining behavioural tendency scores derived from housing and sociodemographic variables adjusting for age, sex, native birth and occupational class. Accounting for London's population increase, researchers found associated reductions with mental health outcomes and antisocial behaviour, on an area-wide basis.

Mental health outcomes related to housing instability are defined as positive associations found with depression, anxiety, stress, suicide or suicide risk as well as strong links to risk behaviours such as drug or alcohol dependency (Hoke and Boen, 2021; Suglia et al., 2011; Vásquez-Vera et al., 2016). These factors are commonly found in self-reported health outcomes. Notably, expectant mothers facing eviction are vulnerable to maternal depression and poor mental health during pregnancy (Carrion et al., 2015; Suglia et al., 2011; Vasquez-Vera et al., 2017). A UK-based study of 18,197 families found poor self-reported health outcomes amongst expectant women, new mothers and babies in households that moved during pregnancy and infancy in comparison to non-movers. Of those who moved 8.6% described their health as 'not good'. Also, 7.2% had moved due to homelessness reporting worse health outcomes (Tunstall et al., 2010).

Hazekamp et al. (2021) carried out a descriptive study using 1,267 urban census tracts from Illinois in 2016 to clarify links between evictions experienced by tenants and unhealthy behaviours defined as <7 hours' sleep, smoking, obesity, lack of leisure time or physical activity using census data as well as research from the Eviction Lab (2023), which records eviction data across the country. After adjustment for confounding variables (race, gender and levels of poverty and education) amongst Black non-Hispanic households across Illinois, there was a higher mean rate of eviction filings (6.3) and a higher eviction rate (2.4) when compared to Hispanic households (2.9 and 1.0, respectively) and White non-Hispanic households (3.2 and 1.5). Unsurprisingly Black non-Hispanic households had higher rates of sleep loss, obesity and smoking than others. The study cannot say for certain whether eviction is a catalyst for unhealthy behaviours or if the reverse is true.

In Vancouver and Melbourne, housing instability was a significant factor in risky behaviours as methamphetamine use increased with homelessness. Habitual users placed themselves at risk of eviction through using rent money to score and being unable to hold down jobs. After eviction, sharing of needles, encouragement or initiation into drug usage amongst homeless shelter residents increased (Chamberlain and Johnson, 2013; Damon et al., 2019; Pilarinos et al., 2017).

Tenants facing eviction in America often make hard economical choices including foregoing healthcare treatment (Coley et al., 2013; Hatch and Yun, 2021; Rutan et al., 2023) and refrain from using accident, emergency or necessary inpatient treatments (Zewde et al., 2019). Homelessness or tenants displaced to poorly maintained accommodation often in worse neighbourhoods with higher levels of crime and deprivation create further pressures on emergency services, healthcare and charity food provision resources, all of which are increasingly being drawn upon to meet the need owing to eviction (Acharya et al., 2022; Moran-McCabe and Burris, 2021).

Homelessness also increases the risk of exposure to communicable diseases. The dispersed often find themselves in overcrowded conditions staying with friends or in homeless shelters (Benfer et al., 2021; Biederman et al., 2022; Chisholm et al., 2022; Hoke and Boen, 2021). According to the UK Health Security Agency (2023), tuberculosis (TB) infection is high amongst homeless people or those living in poor housing conditions within densely populated English urban settings, the highest rates within the population were recorded in Leicester and the London Boroughs of Newham and Brent. Screening of new migrants with high healthcare needs and comparison with GP registrations showed low uptake amongst these groups. Asylum seekers and vulnerable migrants encounter difficulties in registering with a Family Doctor due to language barriers, inability to provide ID or proof of address and lack of knowledge of how to get a Doctors' appointment out of hours. Migrants and asylum seekers are more likely to present to accident and emergency services than most of the general population. Those with high healthcare needs are likely to present to emergency healthcare services with advanced symptoms incurring greater healthcare costs and presenting higher risks to public health (Scott et al., 2022; Stagg et al., 2012).

Those infected who are non-UK-born experience higher rates of homelessness compared to UK-born TB sufferers. Many non-UK-born TB sufferers are asylum seekers with greater mental health needs in comparison to UK-born sufferers who are commonly males with histories of imprisonment and drug or alcohol dependency. Homelessness and overcrowding increase the risk and likelihood of exposure to TB, HIV, and Hepatitis B and C, as well as severe influenza in children (Badiaga et al., 2008; Benfer et al., 2021; Hoke and Boen, 2021).

The mortality rate across England and Wales for babies born ≤2,500 g was 9.1 in 1999 accounting for 62% of infant deaths. In comparison, the mortality rate ≥2500 g was 4.3 (Moser et al., 2003). Few UK studies on socio-economic links between low birth weight (LBW) and very low birth weight (VLBW) (less than 1500 g) examine eviction as a variable, focusing instead upon income, education, marital status, single-family household and local area crime, finding statistically significant results for poor health outcomes in areas of deprivation (Bundred et al., 2003; Dibben et al., 2006). American studies showing strong associations with higher infant mortality risk and LBW, as well as pre-term birth (PTB) and reduced foetal growth, also take account of these variables and include poor housing conditions and insecurity of tenure (Blumenshine et al., 2010; Hazekamp et al., 2020; Hoke and Boen, 2021; Spong et al., 2011). Poorer mental health outcomes, as well as PTB and LBW, developmental delay and behavioural issues, were observed for UK expectant mothers and their children placed in temporary hotel or hostel accommodation (Amery et al., 1995; Tunstall et al., 2010).

Non-Hispanic Black mothers in Chicago subject to eviction filing or displacement are significantly at risk for VLBW. In St. Louis, this was irrespective of access to pre-natal health care. Non-Hispanic Black mothers in Chicago had a mean percentage of 3.2% VLBW compared to 1.3% for Non-Hispanic White mothers and 1.7% for Hispanic mothers. Infants suffered long-term adverse health outcomes leading to prolonged inpatient hospital care, cognitive impairment or delayed development, kidney disease, impaired pulmonary function, high blood pressure and hypertension. These patients are also at risk for long-term educational assistance. All these factors place greater financial burdens on already-financially disadvantaged parents particularly lone parents (Hazekamp et al., 2020).

Harville et al. (2022) found strong associations with LBW across 45 American states using eviction data from 2015. After adjustment for covariates odds of LBW were 12–13% greater within the highest-quartile areas of eviction rates. Conversely whilst insecurity of tenure during pregnancy can lead to poor health outcomes, greater housing mobility and the opportunity to relocate to better accommodation often leads to better health outcomes (Harville et al., 2022; Tunstall et al., 2010); however, LBW in teen mothers was associated strongly with numerous moves during pregnancy and inability to produce breast milk (Carrion et al., 2015; Chisholm et al., 2022). LBW influences social inequalities in long-term health, mortality and life expectancy (Moser et al., 2003). Furthermore, frequent moves and rental arrears were associated with poorer access to maternal healthcare, mistreatment of children and children's inpatient admission as well as adult exposure to sleep loss, high blood pressure and domestic violence (Chisholm et al., 2022; Sandel et al., 2018; Vasquez-Vera et al., 2017).

Children of evicted tenants are at higher risk of being taken into care (Berg and Brannstrom, 2018; Hatch and Yun, 2021) and experience trauma that affects development and long-term physical health and leads to academic decline and disciplinary action in schools. They also experience food insecurity (Benfer et al., 2021; Chisholm et al., 2022; Leifheit et al., 2020; Schwartz, 2020; Sandstrom and Huerta, 2013; Tunstall et al., 2010). Adolescence leading to young adulthood is a significant turning point in life in terms of psychological and financial development; exposure to housing instability in adolescence increases the likelihood of depression in adulthood with lasting effects upon wellbeing and financial status. This may form underlying causal factors impacting on future health (Hatch and Yun, 2021; Hoke and Boen, 2021), including increased risk of cardiovascular and pulmonary disease in later life leading to decreased life expectancy (Benfer et al., 2021; Chisholm et al., 2022; Leifheit et al., 2020; Schwartz, 2020). This is partially attributable to the postponement of medical treatment during periods of housing instability and a general lack of access to healthcare (Hatch and Yun, 2021; Rutan et al., 2023).

Acharya et al. (2022) carried out a retrospective cross-sectional study using census data of tenant households examining associations between self-reported exposure to risk of eviction, anxiety and depression. Covariate details such as education, ethnicity, age, gender and household income were also considered. The prevalence of depression in the overall population (659,071) was 18.2%. But in the population of renting tenants (131,734), the prevalence was 30.9%. Higher rates of anxiety and depression were found amongst those in rental arrears (15,014) 46.4%. The findings showed Black and Hispanic people, those on lower incomes and lower educational attainment were more likely to have rental arrears, in comparison to those with graduate degrees and incomes of $100,000. A separate study by Zewde et al. (2019) reached the same conclusion whilst controlling for poverty and rental burdens.

Between 1991 and 2013, low-income households in the US private rented sector spent over 50% of their income on rent, struggling to balance paying for food, medical care or school supplies (Desmond, 2015), exacerbated by stagnant wages, salary decreases, rental increases and lack of federal financial support (Acharya et al., 2022; Benfer et al., 2021; Hazekamp et al., 2021). Twenty-five per cent of renters on low incomes were found to be spending around 70% of their earnings on rent (Desmond, 2015; Hazekamp et al., 2021) far exceeding the 30% of income spent on rent that the American National Housing Act considers to be an affordable burden (Zewde et al., 2019) leaving families facing choices on limiting expenditure has a negative impact on health development such as cutting down on food, medical care and children's extra-curricular activities. Those on lower incomes are less likely to be insured and when struggling financially are less likely to be able to afford healthcare (Bailey, 2020). Parents feel unable to adequately support children which contributes to children's physiological stress with negative impacts on development and emotional learning (Coley et al., 2013).

Many renters are vulnerable to insecurity of tenure when unforeseen events increase financial hardship such as job loss or sickness. Occupiers often face choices between foregoing the cost of other goods such as healthcare; to pay rent, these choices increasingly place tenants at risk of rental arrears and eviction (Hepburn et al., 2020; Rutan et al., 2023). In the UK, healthcare is free at the point of service but occupiers are faced with similar harsh economic choices over the affordability of rent, heating costs and food this is examined further in the chapters on Unintended Effects and Cost.

References

Acharya, B., Bhatta, D. and Dhakal, C. (2022). 'The Risk of Eviction and the Mental Health Outcomes Among the US Adults', *Preventive Medicine Reports*, 29, p. 101981.

Amery, J., Tomkins, A. and Victor, C. (1995). 'The Prevalence of Behavioural Problems Amongst Homeless Primary School Children in an Outer London Borough: A Feasibility Study', *Public Health*, 109(6), pp. 421–424.

Badiaga, S., Raoult, D. and Brouqui, P. (2008). 'Preventing and Controlling Emerging and Reemerging Transmissible Diseases in the Homeless', *Emerging Infectious Diseases*, 14(9), pp. 1353–1359.

Bailey, P. (2020). *Housing and Health Partners Can Work Together to Close the Housing Affordability Gap*. Washington. DC: Center on Budget and Policy Priorities.

Benfer, E.A., Vlahov, D., Long, M.Y., Walker-Wells, E., Pottenger, J.L., Gonsalves, G. and Keene, D.E. (2021). 'Eviction, Health Inequity, and the Spread of COVID-19: Housing Policy as a Primary Pandemic Mitigation Strategy', *Journal of Urban Health*, 98(1), pp. 1–12.

Berg, L. and Brannstrom, L. (2018). 'Evicted Children and Subsequent Placement in Out-of-Homecare: A Cohort Study', *PLoS One*, 13(4), p. e0195295. Available from: https://doi.org/10.1371/journ al.pone.0195295

Biederman, D.J., Callejo-Black, P., Douglas, C., O'Donohue, H.A., Daeges, M., Sofela, O. and Brown, A. (2022). 'Changes in Health and Health Care Utilization Following Eviction From Public Housing', *Public Health Nursing (Boston, MA)*, 39(2), pp. 363–371.

Blumenshine, P., Egerter, S., Barclay, C.J., Cubbin, C. and Braveman, P.A. (2010). 'Socioeconomic Disparities in Adverse Birth Outcomes: A Systematic Review', *American Journal of Preventive Medicine*, 39(3), pp. 263–272.

Bundred, P., Manning, D., Brewster, B. and Buchan, I. (2003). 'Social Trends in Singleton Births and Birth Weight in Wirral Residents, 1990–2001', *Archives of Disease in Childhood. Fetal and Neonatal Edition*, 88(5), pp. F421–F424.

Carrion, B.V., Earnshaw, V.A., Kershaw, T., Lewis, J.B., Stasko, E.C., Tobin, J.N. and Ickovics, J.R. (2015). 'Housing Instability and Birth Weight Among Young Urban Mothers', *Journal of Urban Health*, 92(1), pp. 1–9.

Chamberlain, C. and Johnson, G. (2013). 'Pathways into Adult Homelessness', *Journal of Sociology (Melbourne, Vic.)*, 49(1), pp. 60–77.

Chisholm, E., Bierre, S., Davies, C. and Howden-Chapman, P. (2022) '"That House was a Home": Qualitative Evidence from New Zealand on the Connections Between Rental Housing Eviction and Poor Health Outcomes', *Health Promotion Journal of Australia*, 33(3), pp. 861–868.

Coley, R.L., Leventhal, T., Lynch, A.D. and Kull, M. (2013, September). *Poor Quality Housing is Tied to Children's Emotional and*

Behavioral Problems. Policy Research Brief, Chicago: MacArthur Foundation.

Damon, W., McNeil, R., Milloy, M.J., Nosova, E., Kerr, T. and Hayashi, K. (2019, March). 'Residential Eviction Predicts Initiation of or Relapse into Crystal Methamphetamine Use Among People Who Inject Drugs: A Prospective Cohort Study', *Journal of Public Health*, 41(1), pp. 36–45.

DeGrazia Jr, R., Abdullahi, A., Mood, M., Diehl, C., Stockwell, I. and Pollack, C.E. (2023). 'Addressing Housing-Related Social Needs for Medicaid Beneficiaries: A Qualitative Assessment of Maryland's Medicaid § 1115 Waiver Program', *BMC Health Services Research*, 23, p. 999.

Desmond, M. (2015). 'Unaffordable America: Poverty, Housing, and Eviction', *Fast Focus: Institute for Research on Poverty*, 22(22), pp. 1–6.

Desmond, M. (2016). *Evicted: Poverty and profit in the American city.* New York, NY: Crown/Archetype.

Desmond, M. (2018). 'Heavy is the House: Rent Burden Among the American Urban Poor', *International Journal of Urban and Regional Research*, 42, pp. 160–170.

Desmond, M. and Kimbro, R.T. (2015) 'Eviction's Fallout: Housing, Hardship, and Health', *Social Forces*, 94(1), pp. 295–324.

Dibben, C., Sigala, M. and Macfarlane, A. (2006). 'Area Deprivation, Individual Factors and Low Birth Weight in England: Is There Evidence of an "Area Effect"?', *Journal of Epidemiology and Community Health (1979)*, 60(12), pp. 1053–1059.

Doran, K., Guzzardo, J., Hill, K., Kitterlin, N., Li, W. and Liebl, R., 2003. *No Time for Justice: A Study of Chicago's Eviction Court.* Chicago: Lawyers' Committee for Better Housing, Chicago-Kent School of Law, Illinois Institute of Technology.

Eviction Lab. (2023). *Eviction Lab Research.* Princeton University. [online]. (updated 10 July 2023). Available from: https://eviction-lab.org/research/

Harville, E.W., Wallace, M.E. and Theall, K.P. (2022) 'Eviction as a Social Determinant of Pregnancy Health: County-Level Eviction Rates and Adverse Birth Outcomes in the United States', *Health & Social Care in the Community*, 30(6), pp. e5579–e5587.

Hatch, M.E. and Yun, J. (2021). 'Losing Your Home Is Bad for Your Health: Short- and Medium-Term Health Effects of Eviction on Young Adults', *Housing Policy Debate*, 31(3–5), pp. 469–489.

Hazekamp, Yousuf, S., Day, K., Daly, M.K., & Sheehan, K. (2020) 'Eviction and Pediatric Health Outcomes in Chicago', *Journal of community health*, 45(5), pp. 891–899. Available at: https://doi.org/10.1007/s10900-020-00806-y.

Hazekamp, C., Yousuf, S., Khare, M. and MacDowell, M. (2021). 'Unhealthy Behaviours in Urban Illinois Communities Affected by Eviction: A Descriptive Analysis', *Health & Social Care in the Community*, 29(3), pp. 867–875.

Hepburn, P., Louis, R., Desmond, M. (2020). Racial and Gender Disparities among Evicted Americans. Eviction Lab Research. Princeton University. (16 December 2020). Available from: https://evictionlab.org/demographics-of-eviction/

Hoke, M.K. and Boen, C.E. (2021) 'The Health Impacts of Eviction: Evidence from the National Longitudinal Study of Adolescent to Adult Health', *Social Science & Medicine (1982)*, 273, p. 113742.

House of Commons Committee of Public Accounts. (2022, January). Written Evidence Submitted by StepChange Debt Charity. PRP0005.

Jacob, Z. (2023). 'A Comparative Analysis of the US and UK Health Care Systems. University of Michigan. Department of Economics', *Michigan Journal of Economics*, 26 May.

Leifheit, K.M., Schwartz, G.L., Pollack, C.E., Black, M.M., Edin, K.J., Althoff, K.N. and Jennings, J.M. (2020). 'Eviction in Early Childhood and Neighborhood Poverty, Food Security, and Obesity in Later Childhood and Adolescence: Evidence from a Longitudinal Birth Cohort', *SSM – Population Health*, 11, p. 100575. Available from: https://doi.org/10.1016/j.ssmph.2020.100575.

Lonegrass, M.T. (2015). 'Eliminating Landlord Retaliation in England and Wales – Lessons From the United States', *Louisiana Law Review*, 75(4), pp. 1071–1123.

Moran-McCabe, K., Burris, S. (2021) 'Eviction and the Necessary Conditions for Health', The New England journal of medicine, 385(16), pp. 1443–1445.

Moser, K., Li, L. and Power, C. (2003). 'Social Inequalities in Low Birth Weight in England and Wales: Trends and Implications for Future Population Health', *Journal of Epidemiology and Community Health (1979)*, 57(9), pp. 687–691.

Oatt, P. (2019). *Selective Licensing: The Basis for a Collaborative Approach to Addressing Health Inequalities*. Abingdon. Oxon: Routledge.

Ozawa, S. (2011). 'Private Health Insurance', in Guinness, L. and Wiseman, V. (Eds), *Introduction to Health Economics*. Second Edition. Maidenhead: McGraw Hill, pp. 160–172.

Petersen, J., Alexiou, A., Brewerton, D., Cornelsen, L., Courtin, E., Cummins, S., Marks, D., Seguin, M., Stewart, J., Thompson, K. and Egan, M. (2022) 'Impact of Selective Licensing Schemes for Private Rental Housing on Mental Health and Social Outcomes in Greater London, England: A Natural Experiment Study', *BMJ Open*, 12(12), pp. e065747.

Pilarinos, A., Kennedy, M.C., McNeil, R., Dong, H., Kerr, T. and Debeck, K. (2017, May 12). 'The Association Between Residential Eviction and Syringe Sharing Among a Prospective Cohort of Street-Involved Youth', *Harm Reduction Journal*, 14, p. 24.

Rudge, J. and Gilchrist, R. (2005). 'Excess Winter Morbidity Among Older People at Risk of Cold Homes: A Population-Based Study in a London Borough', *Journal of Public Health (Oxford, England)*, 27(4), pp. 353–358.

Rutan, D.Q., Hepburn, P. and Desmond, M. (2023, February). 'The Suburbanization of Eviction: Increasing Displacement and Inequality Within American Suburbs', *The Russell Sage Foundation Journal of the Social Sciences*, 9(1), pp. 104–125.

Sandel, M., Sheward, R., Ettinger de Cuba, S., Coleman, S.M., Frank, D.A., Chilton, M., Black, M., Heeren, T., Pasquariello, J., Casey, P., Ochoa, E. and Cutts, D. (2018). 'Unstable Housing and Caregiver and Child Health in Renter Families', *Pediatrics*, 141(2).

Sandstrom, H. and Huerta, S. (2013). *The Negative Effects of Instability on Child Development: A Research Synthesis*, vol. 3. pp. 87–90. Washington. DC.

Sawyer, A., Sherriff, N., Bishop, D., Darking, M. and Huber, J.W. (2022). "It's Changed My Life Not to Have the Continual Worry of Being Warm" – Health and Wellbeing Impacts of a Local Fuel Poverty Programme: A Mixed-Methods Evaluation. *BMC Public Health*, 22, p. 786.

Schwartz, G.L. (2020). *Cycles of Disadvantage: Eviction & Children's Health in the United States* [dissertation]. Boston, Massachusetts: Harvard University. Available from: https://dash. harvard.edu/handle/1/37365869L

Scott, R., Forde, E. and Wedderburn, C. (2022) 'Refugee, Migrant and Asylum Seekers' Experience of Accessing and Receiving Primary Healthcare in a UK City of Sanctuary', *Journal of Immigrant and Minority Health*, 24(1), pp. 304–307.

Shelter. (2021, October 13). *Health of One in Five Renters Harmed by Their Home*. England: Shelter. [online]. Available from: https://england. shelter.org.uk/media/press_release/health_of_one_in_five_renters_ harmed_by_their_home

Spong, C.Y., Iams, J., Goldenberg, R., Hauck, F.R. and Willinger, M. (2011). 'Disparities in Perinatal Medicine: Preterm Birth, Stillbirth, and Infant Mortality', *Obstetrics and Gynecology*, 117(4), pp. 948–955.

Stagg, H.R., Jones, J., Bickler, G. and Abubakar, I. (2012). 'Poor Uptake of Primary Healthcare Registration Among Recent Entrants to the UK: A Retrospective Cohort Study', *BMJ Open*, 2(4).

Suglia, S.F., Duarte, C.S. and Sandel, M.T. (2011). 'Housing Quality, Housing Instability, and Maternal Mental Health', *Journal of Urban Health*, 88(6), pp. 1105–1116.

Tunstall, H., Pickett, K. and Johnsen, S. (2010). 'Residential Mobility in the UK During Pregnancy and Infancy: Are Pregnant Women, New Mothers and Infants 'Unhealthy Migrants'?', *Social Science and Medicine*, 71(4), pp. 786–798.

UK Health Security Agency. (2023, August 3). 'TB Incidence and Epidemiology in England, 2021', *GOV.UK*. [online]. Available from: https://www.gov.uk/government/publications/tuberculosis-in-england-2022-report-data-up-to-end-of-2021/tb-incidence-and-epidemiology-in-england-2021

Vasquez-Vera, H., Palencia, L., Magna, I., Mena, C., Neira, J. and Borrell, C. (2017). 'The Threat of Home Eviction and Its Effects on Health Through the Equity Lens: A Systematic Review', *Social Science and Medicine*, 175, pp. 199–208.

Vásquez-Vera, H., Rodríguez-Sanz, M., Palència, L. and Borrell, C. (2016). 'Foreclosure and Health in Southern Europe: Results from the Platform for People Affected by Mortgages', *Journal of Urban Health*, 93(2), pp. 312–330.

Zewde, N., Eliason, E., Allen, H. and Gross, T. (2019). 'The Effects of the ACA Medicaid Expansion on Nationwide Home Evictions and Eviction-Court Initiations: United States, 2000–2016', *American Journal of Public Health (1971)*, 109(10), pp. 1379–1383.

3 The Effectiveness of Housing Policy Development

In this chapter, the impact of housing policy on tenants, the group of interest, is examined through the lens of effectiveness. Morestin (2012) recognises causal links can take a long time before becoming apparent often shaped by multiple factors. Policy effectiveness is also influenced by implementation. This chapter examines the implementation context as well as intermediate effects likely to have a derived impact on health and wellbeing to ask what the effects of housing policy under study are on tenants' safety in terms of positive, negative and intermediate effects as well as plausibility of the intervention logic.

Abolishing Section 21 was only a small aspect of changes in the now defunct Renters (Reform) Bill (DLUHC, 2023a) which eliminated ASTs, making all tenancies periodic to a maximum of either 28 days or a month, with no end date (Wilson and Cromarty, 2023; Smith, 2023a). Originally, ASTs were implemented under the Housing Act 1988 to reinvigorate a shrinking private rental market which represented less than 10% of England's housing stock (Driscoll, 2006). Through providing security of tenure and rent control provision, the government attracted investment enabling the UK's private rented sector to grow (Lowe and Hughes, 2002). Since that time, the sector's growth has doubled currently representing 19% of the nation's housing stock (MHCLG, 2020a; DLUHC, 2022a). This has reinforced perceptions that introducing ASTs was successful (Lonegrass, 2015) providing guaranteed income for the duration of the term (Propertymark, 2023).

Tenants served with Section 21 notices are classed as being at risk of homelessness within 56 days from notice expiry and are owed a homelessness prevention or relief duty from their local council under the Homelessness Reduction Act (2017). Sixty-seven per cent of landlords surveyed by the DLUHC (2022b) had carried out Section 21 evictions. Twenty-five per cent of tenants were evicted under Section 8

DOI: 10.1201/9781032705071-3

for tenancy agreement breaches. During 2022–2023, much of the increase in demand for homeless duty or increases in landlords' threats of homelessness were strongly associated with tenants nearing the end of an AST affecting 31,320 households with children. A total of 21,530 households AST agreements were not renewed because landlords wanted to sell or re-let the property, representing an increase of 20% from the previous year (DLUHC, 2023c).

Section 4 of the Homelessness Reduction Act (2017) places duties upon local authorities for 56 days to assist in retaining current accommodation or arrange relocation and avoidance of homelessness. The duty ends when accommodation is secured, or applicants are made homeless. Of those families with children owed a relief duty during 2022–2023 the figure increased by 43% compared to the previous year, over half of the landlords in these cases evicted tenants to sell or re-let their properties. Another reason why ASTs ended was due to rental increases affecting 450 households. In comparison during 2021–2022, tenancies ending after rental increases affected 170 households (DLUHC, 2023c). Aside from rental increases or wanting to sell or re-let, tenants surveyed by the Joseph Rowntree Foundation reported Section 21 evictions were carried out in retaliation for making complaints (Clarke et al., 2017). The Department for Communities and Local Government (DCLG, 2015) reported over 80,000 tenants surveyed were evicted in response to complaints about disrepair. When the account is taken of the tenants' families, it is likely that retaliatory eviction effected over 200,000 people that year. A smaller number of tenants incurred arrears because of vulnerability and inability to manage finances, some explained the shortfall difference between rent and housing benefit was impossible to meet from benefit entitlement (Clarke et al., 2017).

Local authorities have a mandatory duty to report data on statutory homelessness. This is collected in a data repository known as the Homelessness Case Level Information Collection (H-CLIC). Between 2022 and 2023, there were 298,430 households at threat of homelessness or already homeless at the time of making an application and owed a homelessness duty representing a 6.8% increase compared to 2021–2022 and also 3% above the pre-COVID level of 2019–2020 (DLUHC, 2023c).

According to the Ministry of Justice (MOJ) (2023), England's overall trend in possession claims, orders and repossessions from private and social landlords declined between 2014 and 2022 (Table 3.1). There is a marked decline in lawful evictions between

Table 3.1 Combined Social and Private Landlord Claims, Orders and Repossessions

Year	Combined private & social landlord claims	All landlord possession orders made	Social landlord claims	Social landlord Repossessions by CC Bailiffs	Private landlord claims	Private landlord Repossessions by CC Bailiffs
2014	123,216	122,000	100,776	19,983 (16%)	22,440	6,197 (5%)
2015	110,347	113,744	90,312	19,095 (17%)	20,035	5,919 (5%)
2016	98,669	103,634	78,991	17,491 (17.7%)	19,678	5,852 (5.9%)
2017	98,460	96,587	77,733	15,697 (15.9%)	20,727	6,098 (6%)
2018	94,091	89,456	71,465	15,504 (16.5%)	22,626	6,715 (7%)
2019	87,880	83,523	64,664	14,452 (16.5%)	23,216	7,070 (8%)
2020	29,620	21,157	17,472	3,334 (11%)	12,148	1,903 (6.5%)
2021	28,961	22,658	13,201	2,996 (10%)	15,760	3,325 (11.5%)
2022	57,987	56,360	27,000	5,528 (9.5%)	24,987	6,997 (12%)
Mean	81,026	78,791	60,179	12,676 (15.6%)	20,180	5,564 (6.9%)

Source: (Ministry of Justice, 2023).

2020 and 2021 owing to the stay on evictions imposed during the COVID-19 pandemic (Justice.gov.uk, 2020a, 2020b). Despite the decline on average across the period, there are three times as many possession claims made by the social housing sector compared to the private rented sector. When figures for social housing and private rented sector claims are taken together, the reduction in social housing claims creates an annual reduction effect in the rate of national claims across both sectors. When separated from social housing claims, the number of annual claims and final possession orders in the private rented sector pre-pandemic between 2016 and 2019 shows a yearly increase. Post-pandemic, the rate of repossessions in the private rented sector has doubled almost returning to the same rate they were in 2019. Similarly, in 2022, the number of lawful evictions within the social rented sector is double that of the rate during the pandemic (MOJ, 2023).

Whilst the past 20 years saw housing quality improvements, 23% of private rented properties failed to meet the decent homes standard in 2019, the equivalent in social rented properties was 12% and 16% for owner-occupied homes (MHCLG, 2020a). The increase in the private rented sector properties over the past 20 years was accompanied with a decrease in social housing properties whilst house prices rose, making it less affordable for first-time buyers. The growth of private renting and the prevalence of the sector's poorer housing conditions such as damp, mould, excess cold and the associated risks to physical and mental health means more resources to enforce and intervene should be directed to remedy defects and sustain a better quality (Egan et al., 2022; Harris and McKee, 2021). The problem is worsened through insecurity of tenure and retaliatory evictions. This together with rental increases and the stress of unaffordability leads indirectly to poor health outcomes whilst alternative accommodation options become more limited within an increasingly unaffordable market (Clair et al., 2019; Harris and McKee, 2021).

Tenant support organisations wanted Section 21 retaliatory evictions abolished (Lonegrass, 2015). The Law Commission (2008) examined the issue but was cautious about the effects of introducing protective laws because many retaliatory evictions already go unchallenged and creating new legislation was deemed unlikely to alter this. The Association of Tenancy Relations Officers (ATRO) urged parliament to consider making retaliation a reasonable defence for tenants facing Section 21 evictions (CLGC, 2013). The Law Commission

(2008) felt the practicalities of being able to prove evictions are motivated by retaliation potentially render such measures ineffective.

The NAO (2021) found that poor funding and lack of training resources have hampered local authorities' ability to train officers. Consequently, many local authorities lack suitably qualified officers with sufficient comprehension of regulatory powers to proactively inspect properties and collect evidence to acceptable standards of proof. Scarcity of choice in the property market leaves many local authorities strongly reliant upon landlords at the lower end of the market to provide temporary accommodation who are less likely to be compliant with housing laws and more likely to leave the market if subject to heavy regulation (Moore, 2023).

The difficulties for local authorities resourcing proactive housing inspections were a motivating factor in developing the Homes (Fitness for Human Habitation) Bill which amends Section 9(a) of the Landlord and Tenant Act 1985 to allow tenants to take private action against negligent landlords (Wilson and Cromarty, 2018). The amendment requires residential properties (including common parts) be 'fit for human habitation' when the tenancy agreement commences and for the duration of the lease. Fitness for Human Habitation is defined under Section 10(1) of the Landlord and Tenant Act (1985) and if one or more of the matters listed are present, the property is unsuitable for occupancy. This criterion covers dilapidation, structural instability, damp, lack of natural light or ventilation, inadequate provisions of hot and cold water, drainage, wastewater disposal, sanitary conveniences and insufficient facilities for food preparation. Section 10(2) of the Landlord and Tenant Act 1985 is also amended to incorporate 'prescribed hazards' as defined by Section 2 of the Housing Act 2004, where hazards are categorised through risk assessment and order of seriousness from Category 1 (the most serious) where there is a mandatory duty for local authorities to enforce to Category 2 hazards which are less serious in nature and for which local authorities have discretionary powers to address. Housing risk assessment of Category 1 or 2 hazards is not essential for proving unfitness but is considered additional evidence sufficiently demonstrated by referring to hazards as set out in the government's operating guidance (ODPM, 2006; Shelter, 2023). In simple cases, a GP letter and photographs are sufficient. Expert evidence can be drawn for more complex cases exploring the extent of unfitness (Peaker and Bates, 2019).

Schedule 1 (35) of the Legal Aid, Sentencing and Punishment of Offenders Act (LASPO) (2012) makes provision of civil legal services for tenants who complain of a deficiency posing a 'serious risk of harm' in a rented property whose responsibility to rectify is that of the landlord. A pre-action protocol exists for these claims from which a claim against the landlord can be made under the Homes (Fitness for Human Habitation) Act 2018 for breach of repairing covenants if that procedure fails, providing the landlord was aware of the issues and had sufficient opportunity to rectify them. The process allows for expedient dispute settlements alternatively through mediation or through landlord complaints procedures at no cost to the tenant and minimal cost to the landlord. In urgent cases, this will result in an order for repair being made against the landlord (Community Law Partnership, 2018; Housing Ombudsman Service, 2021; MOJ, 2021; Peaker and Bates, 2019).

Tenants with income below £2,657 per calendar month (PCM) and savings under £8,000 qualify for legal aid (Housing Law Practitioners Association, 2013) covering costs of the claim and some protection against loss. The procedure does not allow tenants to make damages claims. The extra cost of applying for this together with the disrepair claim is negligible. Being unable to apply for damages disadvantages tenants facing potential losses during the time it takes for the case to go through the courts. The alternative is to obtain representation on a 'No Win No Fee' basis at no risk to the claimant. Damages exceeding £10,000 can also be pursued, regardless of income without requiring proof of health risk (Choudhury, 2018; Community Law Partnership, 2018).

LASPO Act (2012) removed legal aid funding for claims against landlords concerning disrepair and damages. Previously, these types of cases were evaluated by legal firms to ensure cases meet certain legal tests. There is no guarantee cases are now being assessed in this way by 'No Win No Fee' services meaning many claims entering the legal system may be of poor quality (Inside Housing, 2022). Legal aid cuts reduced service provision exacerbating the lack of protection for tenants in England and Wales from 755 offices in 2011–2012 to 322 in 2020–2021 leaving an estimated 40% of the population without access to local housing legal aid provision (Reeve-Lewis et al., 2022).

Conflict theorists disagree that regulation protects vulnerable groups and keeps powerful groups in check because regulation fails when powerful business groups intended to be regulated are involved in shaping these same regulations, laws and policies and are favoured when regulation is implemented, whilst economic concerns are prioritised (Hutter, 1997). Between 2010 and 2020, the Conservative party received around £60.8 million in donations from companies and individuals with large property interests accounting for more than a fifth of donations and higher than donations made to other parties from companies or individuals with similar interests. This was substantially higher than donations made between 2015 and 2019 from the property market which accounted for one in ten pounds worth of donations (HCCPA, 2022).

Reliance on donations of this magnitude from one sector potentially constrains governments from addressing a housing crisis effectively, acting mainly in the interests of this group. This phenomenon is known as policy capture and leads to ineffective regulation and reluctance to prosecute where legislation never goes far enough as regulators wish but is not sufficiently as relaxed as businesses prefer. Low levels of prosecutions are symptomatic of regulatory authorities being poorly resourced, having to administer poorly structured legislation with weak enforcement sanctions (HCCPA, 2022; Hutter, 1997).

Frequent leadership changes make housing policy vulnerable to capture with insufficient measures to safeguard against it because of the frequent turnover of housing ministers – 18 in the last 20 years and changes of secretaries of state every 2 to 2.5 years (HCCPA, 2022). At national and local levels regulatory focuses are politically influenced (Dhesi, 2019; Spencer et al., 2020). A degree of policy capture exists between landlords and local authorities reliant upon private landlords' properties for temporary accommodation of eligible low-income households and a reluctance to prosecute for housing offences, allowing crimes to proliferate through sufferance (Moore, 2023; Spencer et al., 2020). Policy capture is exacerbated by reliance on donations from persons who can influence and shape policy in their own interests (HCCPA, 2022).

Aside from Possession claim statistics recorded by the MOJ, in 2014, it was confirmed through a parliamentary question to the Secretary of State for Communities and Local Government that statistics on annual rates of retaliatory evictions are not recorded (UK Parliament, 2015). The evidence base is weak and data collection and outcome measurement needs improving (Downie, 2018). Safer Renting were openly critical of the English Housing Survey (EHS) which collects tenants' data sporadically and inconsistently. An example given is that

1.7% of tenants surveyed stated their relationship with their landlord was poor whilst 8.3% were asked to leave – no information is provided on whether departure was facilitated by lawful means. Further, 6.5% stated they were 'dissatisfied' with the 'service of their landlord' but no reasons are given as to why (MHCLG, 2020b; Reeve-Lewis et al., 2022). In November 2022, Shelter reported almost a quarter of private renters (2.8m) and 504,000 private tenants experiencing eviction threats or who received eviction notices in the past month were all struggling to pay rent (Shelter, 2022).

In written evidence to the Communities and Local Government Committee (CLGC), the ATRO raised concerns that local authorities seldom use available powers under the Protection from Eviction Act 1977 sufficiently well to address harassment and illegal eviction incidents perpetrated by a minority of criminal landlords (CLGC, 2013). This poor response is partly attributable to low staffing owing to austerity measures, for example in recent years, the employment of tenancy relations officers was reduced leaving fewer officers in post with the requisite skills (Spencer et al., 2020).

Enforcement under Section 6 of the Protection from Eviction Act is a discretionary power leaving under-resourced councils with little incentivisation to pursue (Reeve-Lewis et al., 2022; Spencer et al., 2020). The past 20 years have seen poor governmental support and guidance towards local authorities' efforts to protect tenants. It is a further contributory factor to de-prioritisation of these types of local government investigations (CLGC, 2013; Spencer et al., 2020).

A Freedom of Information request to the Metropolitan Police (2022) asked how many illegal eviction incidents were investigated between 2018 and 2021. The response showed a total of 66 cases, averaging around 16.5 per annum. Between 2013 and 2020, MOJ data recorded 334 cases of offences under the Protection from Eviction Act 1977 and 154 cases (46%) resulted in convictions. This indicator underestimates the scale of the problem because it only quantifies where Local Authorities are willing to enforce. In 2021, it was recorded by Parliament that almost 50% of prosecutions carried out for unlawful eviction and harassment over the past three years were undertaken in South Yorkshire and by the Metropolitan Police. (Metropolitan Police, 2022; UK Parliament, 2021).

Spencer et al. (2020) found obstacles to enforcing against illegal evictions relate to the 'nature and scale' of criminality in the private rented sector and difficulties reconciling this with complex regulations where vague wording is inadequately constructed to address typically encountered criminal situations. This is examined further in the chapter on unintended effects.

The removal of Section 21 under the Renters (Reform) Bill (DLUHC, 2023a) was to have been accompanied by amendments to possession Ground 1 which currently facilitates gaining possession for the property to become the main home of a landlord, their spouse, civil partner, or close family members. Ground 1(a) expanded this to include a provision for landlords wishing to sell. After an eviction, the landlord would have been prohibited from advertising the property for rent or letting it for three months (Cummins, 2023; Wilson and Cromarty, 2023).

The bill also contained, a mandatory ground concerning rental arrears where notice could be served if a tenant incurs at least two months' arrears on three separate occasions across a three-year period (DLUHC, 2023c; Wilson and Cromarty, 2023). Restrictions would have been imposed on rental increases, landlords would only be able to do this annually being unable to enforce any contractual rent review clauses to the contrary (Wilson and Cromarty, 2023). Tenants would have been able to contest rental increases before the First-tier property tribunal (Cummins, 2023; DLUHC, 2023b; Smith, 2023a).

In Wales, a similar national registration scheme launched in 2015 exists in parallel with other types of housing enforcement such as selective licensing (Welsh Government, 2018).

The compatibility of the Renters (Reform) Bill's database and property portal with local authority selective licensing schemes would have enabled these resources to function jointly in targeting resources to regulate unlicensed properties (Chartered Institute of Environmental Health (CIEH), 2023). The Large Agents Representation Group (LARG) (2023) believe all the information for enforcement purposes supplant the need for selective licensing and called for it to be scrapped. But neither a Landlord database or the Rent Smart Wales scheme replace the regulatory functions of selective licensing which enables local authorities to proactively enforce the private rented sector using a multiagency approach without reliance upon responding only to tenants' complaints. Licensing income enables local authorities to fund staffing, enforcement and training and obligates licence holders to operate to a minimum set of standards regulating waste management, overcrowding, gas, fire and electrical safety with the derived benefit of positively impacting health through these standards by protecting vulnerable tenants and reducing levels of crime and anti-social behaviour in the rental sector (CIEH, 2023; Oatt, 2019; Petersen et al., 2022). Rent Smart Wales like the Renters (Reform) Bill has a focus on regulating landlords' marketing, letting and management of tenancies. Both schemes rely upon agreeing terms with tenants set down in signed agreements (Renters (Reform) Bill, 2023; Welsh Government, 2018). Like Rent Smart Wales, the Renters (Reform) Bill sought to complement other types of legislation without seeking to overlap or duplicate (DLUHC, 2023b; Wilson and Cromarty, 2023).

Through an amendment to the Housing Act 2004 via Schedule 3 of the Regulatory Enforcement and Sanctions Act 2008, there has always been a provision to create a Primary Authority to oversee Housing Health and Safety Rating System (HHSRS) regulation. To date, this has not happened in housing regulation (Battersby and Pointing, 2019) but is a feature of food safety regulation whereby a business enters a Primary Authority agreement with one Local Authority that oversee enforcement of these companies' standards across all their national business outlets (Tombs, 2016). The Primary Authority enables a coordinated strategy in partnership with stakeholders. Regulatory duties over these actors are third parties all working to a shared goal of compliance. It was envisioned that Primary Authority agreements could be established in housing regulation with landlords who have large portfolios across different local authorities (Battersby and Pointing, 2019).

Both the now defunct Renters (Reform) Bill and Rent Smart Wales seek to ensure registered landlords are sufficiently informed of legal duties and relevant legislative changes. The schemes allow local authorities oversight of all registered landlord details and the locations of their rental properties, with publicly accessible information. For the Renters (Reform) Bill, this was by means of the Property Portal a resource for local authorities use when targeting enforcement activities for breaches of requirements under the bill and issuing civil financial penalties of up to £5,000 for most initial offences and up to £30,000 for ongoing or second offences (DLUHC, 2023b; Welsh Government, 2018; Wilson and Cromarty, 2023). Had the Renters (Reform) Bill progressed, making all tenancies periodic this would have made all fixed-term tenancies unlawful, an offence for which local authorities can take enforcement action (Smith, 2023a; Wilson and Cromarty, 2023).

This is intended to prevent demands for rents to be paid in advance, for example, quarterly or half-yearly. Tenants will also be able to end the tenancy with two months' notice (Cummins, 2023; Smith, 2023b).

The Renters (Reform) Bill (2023) would have taken the Primary Authority idea a step further making provisions for appointing a lead enforcement authority to oversee regulation across all landlords within the property portal. The Lead Authority purpose was to provide uniformity in regulation and disseminate guidance and good enforcement practices to other authorities. Through provisions to enable local authorities to enforce Regulatory (Reform) compliance in other neighbouring authorities, there was potential to provide back-up support for their enforcement activities, particularly where those local authorities lack capacity or expertise (Wilson and Cromarty, 2023).

Housing policy implementation allowed sectoral growth positively ensuring at least six months security of tenure through an AST. The implausible intervention logic of allowing no-fault evictions and rental increases is flawed undermining tenancies by facilitating frequent occupancy changes. Rental increases widen gaps between affordability and rent placing increasing demand upon homeless duty provision. Policy is vulnerable to capture and influence by stakeholders profiting from this situation.

Although the Renters (Reform) Bill (2023) was killed off by dissolution of parliament to call a general election (Cobbold, 2024), the bill highlighted the need for more enforcement consistency, and this is discussed further in the chapter on feasibility and acceptability. Where enforcement failed to reduce hazards and protect health, intermediate provisions of civil remedies were undermined by legal aid cuts restricting repair and damage claims. The bill was drafted whilst knowing that retaliatory eviction data and its causes are poorly collected and evaluated. The property portal would have provided a data collection source for information sharing amongst local authorities, but should reformation of the private rented sector be enacted in a successive parliament; such a database will not supplant other regulatory needs.

References

Battersby, S. and Pointing, J. (2019). *Statutory Nuisance and Residential Property: Environmental Health Problems in Housing.* Abingdon, Oxon: Routledge.

Chartered Institute of Environmental Health (CIEH). (2023, November). Written Evidence. House of Commons Public Bill Committee. Renters (Reform) Bill. RRB50.

Choudhury, A. (2018, October 5). *Can I get Legal Aid for a Legal Housing Disrepair Claim?* Hodhe Jones & Allen. [online]. Available from: https://www.hja.net/expert-comments/blog/housing-help/can-i-get-legal-aid-for-a-legal-housing-disrepair-claim/

Clair, A., Reeves, A., McKee, M. and Stuckler, D. (2019). 'Constructing a Housing Precariousness Measure for Europe', *Journal of European Social Policy*, 29(1), pp. 13–28.

Clarke, A., Hamilton, C., Jones, M. and Muir, K. (2017). *Poverty, Evictions and Forced Moves*. Joseph Rowntree Foundation. (July 2017, updated 3 August 2017). Available from: https://www.jrf.org.uk/report/poverty-evictions-and-forced-moves

Cobbold, N. (2024 May 31). Renters (Reform) Bill dead. Reapit. Available at; https://www.reapit.com/content-hub/renters-reform-bill-dead

Communities and Local Government Committee. (2013, January). *Written Evidence Submitted by the Association of Tenancy Relations Officers*. London: Commons Select Committees.

Community Law Partnership. (2018, June 25). 'Review of the Legal Aid, Sentencing and Punishment of Offenders Act 2012. ("LASPOA")', *communitylawpartnership.co.uk*. [online]. Available from: https://www.communitylawpartnership.co.uk/news/review-of-the-legal-aid-sentencing-and-punishment-of-offenders-act-2012-laspoa

Cummins, S. (2023, June 28). *Renters (Reform) Bill: Key Provisions, Implications for Landlords & Tenants*. Anthony Gold Solicitors. [online]. Available from: https://anthonygold.co.uk/latest/blog/renters-reform-bill

Department for Communities and Local Government. (2015, March). *Review of Property Conditions in the Private Rented Sector Government Response*. London: DCLG.

Department for Levelling Up, Housing and Communities. (2022a, December). *English Housing Survey Headline Report 2021–22*. London: DLUHC.

Department for Levelling Up, Housing and Communities. (2022b, May 11). *Government to Deliver 'New Deal' for Renters*. London: DLUHC.

Department for Levelling Up, Housing and Communities. (2023a, May 17). Renters (Reform) Bill 308-2022-23 (as introduced) UK Parliament. Parliamentary Bills. [online]. Available from: https://publications.parliament.uk/pa/bills/cbill/58-03/0308/220308.pdf

Department for Levelling Up, Housing and Communities. (2023b, May 17). 'Guide to the Renters (Reform) Bill', *GOV.UK*. [online]. Available from: https://www.gov.uk/guidance/guide-to-the-renters-reform-bill

Department for Levelling Up, Housing and Communities. (2023c, October 13). *Statutory Homelessness in England: Financial Year 2022–23*. London: DLUHC.

Dhesi, S. (2019). *Tackling Health Inequalities: Reinventing the Role of Environmental Health*. First Edition. London: Routledge.

Downie, M. ed. (2018). Everybody in: How to End Homelessness in Great Britain. *Crisis*.

Driscoll, J. (2006). *Housing: The New Law: A Practical Guide to the Housing Act 2004*. UK: Butterworths.

Egan, M., Rinaldi, C., Petersen, J., Seguin, M. and Marks, D. (2022). 'Embedding Research on Public Health and Housing into Practice', in Stewart, J. and Moffatt, R. (Eds), *Regulating the Privately Rented Housing Sector*. Abingdon, Oxon: Routledge, pp. 97–105.

Harris, J. and McKee, K. (2021). *Health and Wellbeing in the Private Rented Sector Part 1: Literature Review and Policy Analysis*. UK Collaborative Centre for Housing Evidence, p. 25.

Homelessness Reduction Act 2017 c.13. Available from: https://www.legislation.gov.uk/ukpga/2017/13/contents/enacted

Homes (Fitness for Human Habitation) Act 2018 c.34. Available from: https://www.legislation.gov.uk/ukpga/2018/34/enacted   (accessed 22 October 2023).

House of Commons Committee of Public Accounts. (2022, January). Written Evidence Submitted by Transparency International UK. PRP0007.

Housing Act 1988 c.50. Available from: https://www.legislation.gov.uk/ukpga/1988/50/contents

Housing Act 2004 c.34. Available from: https://www.legislation.gov.uk/ukpga/2004/34/contents

Housing Law Practitioners Association. (2013). *A Guide to Legal Aid & Housing from April 2013*. 2013/05. [online]. Available from: https://www.hlpa.org.uk/cms/wp-content/uploads/2013/05/A-Guide-to-Legal-Aid.doc

Housing Ombudsman Service. (2021, October). *Guidance on Pre-Action Protocol for Housing Conditions Claims and Service Complaints*. [online]. Available from: https://www.housing-ombudsman.org.uk/landlords-info/guidance-notes/guidance-on-pre-action-protocol-for-housing-conditions-claims-and-service-complaints/

Hutter, B. (1997). *Compliance: Regulation and Environment*. Oxford: Clarendon.

Inside Housing. (2022, April 5). 'What is Behind the Rising Number of Disrepair Claims Being Bought Against Social Landlords?', *The Housing Podcast*. [Podcast].

Justice.gov.uk. (2020a). *Practice Direction 51Z: Stay of Possession Proceedings, Coronavirus*. [online]. (updated 11 June 2020). Available from: https://www.justice.gov.uk/courts/procedure-rules/civil/rules/part51/practice-direction-51z-stay-of-possession-proceedings,-coronavirus

Justice.gov.uk. (2020b, July 17). *Practice Direction 55C – Coronavirus: Temporary Provision in Relation to Possession Proceedings*. [online]. Available from: https://www.judiciary.uk/wp-content/uploads/2020/07/CPR-123rd-PD-Update-PD55C-SIGNED.pdf

Landlord and Tenant Act 1985 c.70. Available from: https://www.legislation.gov.uk/ukpga/1985/70

Large Agents Representation Group (LARG). (2023, November). Written Evidence. House of Commons Public Bill Committee. Renters (Reform) Bill. RRB17.

The Law Commission. (2008, August 14). Housing: Encouraging Responsible Letting. LC312. [online]. Available from: https://www.lawcom.gov.uk/project/housing-encouraging-responsible-letting/

Legal Aid, Sentencing and Punishment of Offenders Act 2012 c.10. Available from: https://www.legislation.gov.uk/ukpga/2012/10/contents/enacted (accessed 22 October 2023).

Lonegrass, M.T. (2015) 'Eliminating Landlord Retaliation in England and Wales – Lessons from the United States', *Louisiana Law Review*, 75(4), pp. 1071–1123.

Lowe, S. and Hughes, D. eds. (2002). *The Private Rented Sector in a New Century: Revival or False Dawn?* Bristol University Press: Policy Press.

Marsh, A., Forrest, R., Kennett, P., Niner, P. and Cowan, D. (2000). *Harassment and Unlawful Eviction of Private Rented Sector Tenants and Park Home Residents*. University of Bristol Law School: Department of Environment, Transport and the Regions.

Metropolitan Police. (2022, June, 19). 'Investigations of Accusations of Illegal Evictions on Private Tenants from 2018 to 2021'. Freedom of Information Request Reference No: 01.FOI.22.024106', www.met.police.uk. [online]. Available from: https://www.met.police.uk/foi-ai/af/accessing-information/published-items/?q=Investigations%20of%20Accusations%20of%20Illegal%20Evictions%20on%20Private%20Tenants%20from%202018%20to%202021

Ministry of Housing, Communities and Local Government. (2020a). *English Housing Survey: Headline Report 2019–2020*. London: MHCLG.

Ministry of Housing, Communities and Local Government. (2020b/2021, July 8). *English Housing Survey 2019 to 2020. Annex Tables 3.7 and 3.11*. London: MHCLG.

Ministry of Justice. (2021). *Pre-Action Protocol for Housing Conditions Claims (England)*. (19 August 2021). Justice.gov.uk. [online]. Available from: https://www.justice.gov.uk/courts/procedure-rules/civil/protocol/prot_hou

Ministry of Justice. (2023, February 9). 'Mortgage and Landlord Possession Statistics: October to December 2022', *Gov.UK*. [online]. Available from: https://www.gov.uk/government/statistics/mortgage-and-landlord-possession-statistics-october-to-december-2022

Moore, H. (2023). *The families stuck living in Britain's unlicensed bedsits*. [Today in Focus] (20 November 2023).

Morestin, F. (2012, September). *A Framework for Analyzing Public Policies: Practical Guide*. National Collaborating Centre for Healthy Public Policy. [online]. Available from: http://www.ncchpp.ca/docs/Guide_framework_analyzing_policies_En.pdf

National Audit Office. (2021, December 10). *Regulation of Private Renting: HC 863*. London: Department for Levelling Up, Housing & Communities.

Oatt, P. (2019). *Selective Licensing: The Basis for a Collaborative Approach to Addressing Health Inequalities*. Abingdon. Oxon: Routledge.

Office of the Deputy Prime Minister. (2006, February). *Housing Health and Safety Rating System Operating Guidance*. London: ODPM.

Peaker, G., Bates, J. (2019, February). 'Homes (Fitness for Human Habitation) Act 2018: The Legal Right to a Home Fit to Live In', *lag.org.uk*. [online]. Available from: https://www.lag.org.uk/article/206050/homes-fitness-for-human-habitation-act-2018-the-legal-right-to-a-home-fit-to-live-in

Petersen, J., Alexiou, A., Brewerton, D., Cornelsen, L., Courtin, E., Cummins, S., Marks, D., Seguin, M., Stewart, J., Thompson, K. and Egan, M. (2022) 'Impact of Selective Licensing Schemes for Private Rental Housing on Mental Health and Social Outcomes in Greater London, England: A Natural Experiment Study', *BMJ Open*, 12(12), p. e065747.

Propertymark. (2023, November). Written Evidence. House of Commons Public Bill Committee. Renters (Reform) Bill. RRB48.

Protection from Eviction Act 1977 c.43. Available from: https://www.legislation.gov.uk/ukpga/1977/43

Reeve-Lewis, B., Bolton, J.L. and Rugg, J. (2022, May). *Offences Under the Protection from Eviction Act 1977 in England and Wales: A Report from Safer Renting*. London: Safer Renting. Cambridge House.

Renters (Reform) Bill. (2023, December 7). Department for Levelling Up, Housing and Communities. House of Commons.

Shelter. (2022, June 10). 'Revenge Eviction If You Ask for Repairs', *england.shelter.org*. [online]. Available from: https://england.shelter.org.uk/housing_advice/repairs/revenge_eviction_if_you_ask_for_repairs

Shelter. (2023). 'Fitness for Habitation in Rented Homes', *england. shelter.org.* [online]. (updated 22 June 2023). Available from: https://england.shelter.org.uk/professional_resources/legal/ housing_conditions/responsibility_for_repairs/fitness_for_ habitation_in_rented_homes

Smith, D. (2023a, May 17). *Renters' Reform Finally Arrives.* JMW Solicitors LLP. [online]. Available from: https://www.jmw.co.uk/ blog/commercial-litigation-dispute-resolution/renters-reform-finally-arrives

Smith, D. (2023b, June 1). *Rent Under the Renters (Reform) Bill and Backdoor Rent Control.* JMW Solicitors LLP. [online]. Available from: https://www.jmw.co.uk/blog/commercial-litigation-dispute-resolution/ rent-under-the-renters-reform-bill-and-backdoor-rent

Spencer, R., Reeve-Lewis, B., Rugg, J. and Barata, E. (2020). *Journeys in the Shadow Private Rented Sector.* Cambridge House/Centre for Housing Policy, p. 47.

Tombs, S. (2016, April 14). *'Better Regulation': Better for Whom?* London: Centre for Crime and Justice Studies. [online]. Available from: https://www.crimeandjustice.org.uk/sites/crimeandjustice. org.uk/files/Better%20regulation%20briefing%2C%20April%20 2016_0.pdf

UK Parliament. (2015). *Private Rented Housing: Evictions: Written Question – 212213.* [online]. Available from: http://www.par liament.uk/written-questions-answers-statements/written-ques tion/commons/2014-10-28/212213 Archived at; https://perma.cc/ 9DRM-SWR7

UK Parliament. (2021). *Written Questions, Answers and Statements. Protection from Eviction Act 1977: Prosecutions.* UIN HL13982. [online]. (tabled 8 March 2021). Available from: https://questions-statements.parliament.uk/written-questions/detail/2021-03-08/ HL13982

Welsh Government. (2018). *Evaluation of Rent Smart Wales.* Cardiff: Welsh Government.

Wilson, W. and Cromarty, H. (2018, December 14). *The Homes (Fitness for Human Habitation) Bill 2017–19.* House of Commons Library. [online]. Available from: https://commonslibrary.parlia ment.uk/research-briefings/cbp-8185/

Wilson, W. and Cromarty, H. (2023, October 21). *Research Briefing: Renters (Reform) Bill 2022–23: CBP08756.* London: House of Commons Library.

4 The Unintended Effects of Housing Policy Implementation

In this chapter, unintended effects of policy implementation are examined to determine whether these are positive or negative and how the effects of the latter can be mitigated. According to Morestin (2012), these effects are often influenced by externalities for which there is often no mechanism of control available within the policies being implemented.

Citizens Advice Newcastle and Gatesehead (2023) felt that the Renters (Reform) Bill disproportionately favoured landlords' interests ahead of considering safety measures for tenants. Tenant engagement with government surveys is lower than landlords' input exacerbating issues with policy capture. Tenants' responses show future policy work requires better engagement with all interested parties to better understand perceived complexities around periodic and fixed-term tenancy legislation (HCCPA, 2022a; MHCLG, 2018). Any threat to the security of tenure makes tenants reluctant to complain about disrepair or challenge rental increases for fear of retaliatory eviction. It is not dissimilar in illegal eviction cases; tenants are reluctant to attend court, give evidence or sign statements. Frequent moves create disruption to children's education and for the avoidance of upheaval, tenants prefer to tolerate poor property standards rather than complain (MHCLG, 2018; Reeve et al., 2022; Wilson et al., 2022).

Tenants, when surveyed, felt a proposed three-year tenancy model was preferable to short-term agreements but also acknowledged longer tenancies could restrict their ability to move if circumstances change (DLUHC, 2022; MHCLG, 2018). A few years later when asked for views on fixed-term tenancies of six months minimum without rental increases, tenants felt these were tenure secure (DLUHC, 2022).

DOI: 10.1201/9781032705071-4

Section 33 of the Deregulation Act (2015) was enabled to prevent 'no-fault evictions' being used in retaliation for tenant complaints about disrepair. Providing local authority inspectors had risk
assessed the disrepair under the Housing Act 2004 identifying either
serious Category 1 hazards or lesser Category 2 hazards, and a 'relevant notice' was served. Providing all these conditions are met, a
Section 21 notice is invalid for a period of six months (Battersby and
Pointing, 2019).

Government surveys of tenant representative groups such as Generation Rent, Shelter, Association of Community Organizations for
Reform Now (ACORN) and Citizens Advice all approved the Deregulation Act protection but felt the impact was limited owing to the
complexities in applying protection and because tenants are largely
unaware of the strategy (HCCPA, 2022b; MHCLG, 2018). According to the Community Law Partnership (2018), serving a relevant
notice does little to protect tenants already served with retaliatory
Section 21's prior to a local authorities' involvement. Furthermore,
for Section 21 to be valid, the landlord must demonstrate they have
responded to the complaint adequately within 14 days. If a landlord
fails to do this, provisions under Section 33(2)(b) of Deregulation Act
2015 invalidate the Section 21 notice. Section 33(2)(e) makes a provision to invalidate Section 21 if issued during the period after the complaint was made and before the relevant notice was served (Shelter,
2022). In practice serving, a relevant notice invalidates the Section 21
notice for six months, irrespective of whether it was already issued,
or if it is issued after notification of an inspection. All of this holds up
providing occupiers have previously complained to a landlord in writing and the landlord has had at least two weeks to respond but failed to
do so (Battersby and Pointing, 2019). The timing and precision of all
these elements make for a complex process. An unintended effect of
this measure is that councils often avoid negotiating these hurdles by
simply using other types of action or notices not considered to be relevant notices under the Deregulation Act leaving tenants unprotected
from Section 21 retaliatory evictions (HCCPA, 2022b).

Should section 21 be abolished, the Deregulation Act and all its
complexities will no longer be an issue. But without Section 21, Rugg
and Wallace (2021) warn the obligation upon landlords to use other
measures that require justification is likely to create even more reluctance amongst landlords to let to tenants on lower incomes if they
perceive potential delays in being able to recover their property when

occupiers accrue arrears or behave anti-socially. Furthermore, restricting a landlord's options to evict could have the unintended effect of increasing the number of illegal evictions (Spencer and Rugg, 2023).

Proving harassment under the Protection from Eviction Act is often misunderstood (Reeve-Lewis et al., 2022). It is a defence in law the landlord had 'reasonable cause to believe' the occupant vacated the property, or the landlord had 'reasonable grounds' to withdraw services. There are two applicable tests when considering the offences: firstly, the perpetrators' actions are 'likely' to be causative of the occupier's departure, and secondly, harassment from 'any other person' must be able to evidence an intent to cause the person to leave the property. According to Marsh et al. (2000), opinion amongst enforcers, lawyers, landlords and tenants is divided into what constitutes harassment and the degree to which it is tolerated is contextual. It is broadly agreed that if such actions cause tenants' discomfort and desire to leave in accord with the intent of the perpetrator, this meets the harassment test under the act.

Misinterpretations of law often occur owing to misunderstandings regarding differences between civil and criminal law amongst lay persons embroiled in landlord and tenant disputes and the intervention role of the police. According to Clarke (2020), confusion occurs when members of the public feel a 'moral entitlement' such as a landlord seeking to gain possession of 'their property', without realising the law may not be on their side. In landlord and tenant disputes both parties argue their opponents' actions are unlawful and seek legal intervention from the police. In those circumstances, being told the matter is civil or private and should be resolved in court is difficult to accept. The matter becomes more confusing when the police side with a landlord to evict a tenant. This occurs because the police lack clarity over their own ability to intervene in an unlawful eviction. An example of a recent case (Enwerem v Montague and Delucter Ltd and Bility, 2023) is outlined in the next chapter on equitability.

The Protection from Eviction Act 1977 is a discretionary legislative tool poorly enforced by local authorities (CLGC, 2013; Reeve et al., 2022). Local authority funding was cut in real terms by 49.1% between 2010 and 2018 reducing local government spending power and capacity by 28.6% (NAO, 2019). Most local authorities deployed the bulk of allocated funding towards preserving statutory functions over discretionary ones with a stronger focus on social care over other areas such as housing which as a proportion of funding fell by 52.8% in real terms. Whilst there may be sound economic reasons for imposing cuts, it has negative effects on the local authority's incentive to regulate, undermining their efforts to proactively enforce against landlords and agents and uphold housing and property management standards (Sagoe et al., 2020).

Reeve et al. (2022) felt local authorities would be more incentivised to prosecute for illegal eviction by establishing an alternative civil financial penalty mechanism to fine landlords and recover costs. This was to have been addressed under the Renters (Reform) Bill by enabling local authorities to issue civil financial penalties of up to £30,000 as an alternative to prosecution amending the act where it is evidenced beyond a reasonable doubt that a tenant was harassed or unlawfully evicted (DLUHC, 2023a; Wilson and Cromarty, 2023).

For tenants facing eviction finding accommodation was reported to be problematic, either local properties were unaffordable or landlords were reluctant to let to tenants on housing benefit (Clarke et al., 2017). The scarcity of affordable accommodation for single families in receipt of benefits notably in East London has seen numerous temporary accommodations sourced in shared bedsits, known as House in Multiple Occupation (HMO) traditionally provided for single renters sharing bathroom and kitchen facilities (Moore, 2023). There is no guarantee these properties are safe or compliant; many require property licenses but remain unlicensed raising concerns about the quality of the landlords' managerial oversight. Furthermore, being placed by the local authority into inadequate accommodation can be a deterrent for occupiers to seek help fearing that the local authority will be unable to offer anything better (Moore, 2023; Spencer et al., 2020; Spencer and Rugg, 2023).

Glass Door (HCCPA, 2022d) highlighted the practice of some landlords who still accept benefit recipients obtaining tenant signatures on agreements pre-dated a month earlier than the actual start date to ensure receipt of rent in advance because Universal Credit is paid in arrears. There were also accounts of landlords pressurising tenants not to fill in change of circumstances forms (i.e. starting a job or changing address) to ensure they keep receiving benefit payments.

Housing benefit is also paid in arrears, placing tenants permanently behind on rent (Wilson, 2023). Concerns over unpaid or delayed payments, or difficulties recovering rent, made 37% of agents and 52% of landlords surveyed unwilling to rent to tenants on Housing Benefit. Forty-seven per cent of landlords and 33% of agents expressed similar views regarding tenants on Universal Credit (MHCLG, 2019). Mortgage lenders perceiving benefit-dependent tenants as high-risk impose conditions on buy-to-let mortgages preventing landlords from renting to this group (Reis, 2019). This exclusion creates a market of 'unmet need' for criminal landlords to exploit, a 'shadow rented sector' where unlawful evictions and harassment are commonplace (Spencer et al., 2020).

Non-payment of rent is the biggest risk factor for eviction amongst vulnerable tenants (Tsai and Huang, 2019). Many UK evictions involving arrears are caused by delayed benefit payments brought about by changes in circumstances, often job loss or reduction of hours or taking time off to care for sick children. These changes often lead to administrative delays in payments: some tenants are unable to provide necessary paperwork or have claimed paperwork was lost by benefit staff (Clarke et al., 2017). Agents felt if benefits were paid directly to them in advance as opposed to being paid to the tenant in arrears, they would be more amenable to letting to tenants in receipt of benefits (MHCLG, 2019).

Concerns regarding low enforcement action taken to protect tenants from eviction or harassment extend beyond physical acts of displacement to concerns regarding psychological effects that regular harassment through threats and intimidation play, instilling fear and preying on an occupier's mind. For example, they could return home only to find the locks have been changed. This type of treatment is typical of the worse end of the poor treatment of tenants regularly seen by ATRO members (CLGC, 2013).

Between 1991–1997 a longitudinal cohort study sampling 5,500 British households showed tenants most likely to fall into arrears with an increased risk of eviction were families on low incomes, unemployed and more likely to be in poor health (Böheim and Taylor, 2000). Scarcity of choice of rental accommodation for those at risk of falling into arrears increases the risk of homelessness, unemployment and a spiral into a cycle of poverty (Böheim and Taylor, 2000; Clarke et al., 2017; HCCPA, 2022d; Tsai et al., 2020; Wilson, 2023).

Amidst shortages of affordable housing in urbanised areas, an American observational study assessing housing, psychosocial status and mental health outcomes of 121 adult tenants in rental arrears or tenancy breaches subject to New Haven, Connecticut's, court eviction process found 53.7% of participants earn below $15,000 per annum with rents averaging at $800 per month. About 18–24% of participants in follow-up reported continual struggles to pay rent. There were also a number who decreased monthly rental payments which are most likely associated with poorer quality housing. Most participants post-hearing experienced homelessness or housing instability of at least 20 days out of the 90-day period of follow-up (Tsai et al., 2020).

The Joseph Rowntree Foundation in England interviewed 145 private rented sector tenants mostly female aged between 25 and 54, unable to work or in receipt of benefits and experiencing eviction or forced moves. 43 participants were already evicted and seeking accommodation, 10 were homeless. Another 24 tenants were housed by local authorities in temporary accommodation, often undersized for family provision. Lack of sufficient space and concerns about insecurity of tenure contributed to mental and physical health outcomes. These stressors made it difficult for tenants to engage with support services. Children also suffered as a result and some struggling parents lost custody (Clarke et al., 2017). For these reasons, Tsai et al. (2020) argue eviction itself creates more housing instability amongst those dispersed.

Evictions can adversely affect health inducing depression in those displaced up to at least two years later (Desmond and Kimbro, 2019; Tsai and Huang, 2019). In an earlier study, Desmond (2012) found occupiers spending up to 80% of their income on rent. Any hospitalisation or reduction in work hours left them vulnerable to falling into arrears.

Tsai et al. (2020) found eviction court procedures fail to consider support with housing issues and prevention measures to reduce the likelihood of tenants returning to court for repeated evictions. This presents an opportunity for outreach intervention post-court appearance or during mediation to address ongoing unresolved psychosocial factors and disrupt cycles of repeated evictions. Tsai and Huang (2019) concluded interventions providing aid with debt management, emergency loans, assistance with financial planning and legal advice were reasonably successful in eviction prevention.

The UK government acknowledges inherent difficulties establishing causality and risk factors for homelessness particularly where associations exist with alcohol, substance abuse and mental illness which function as either triggers or consequential risk factors of homelessness. Triggers are acknowledged to be job loss, crime, leaving institutions and mental health deterioration. Family or relationship conflicts are identified as both a trigger and a risk factor (DCLG, 2012). At the individual or population level, 'biological stress-response' is a commonly identified factor which elevates hormonal activity in blood circulation increasing the risk of disease dependent on susceptibility and person's greater or lesser ability to self-care. Stressful events triggered by unaffordable housing, threat of homelessness, forced relocation and loss of wealth can trigger guilt, frustration, aggression, anxiety and shame, and financial strain from being in arrears (Downing, 2016; Ross and Squires, 2011; Turunen and Hiilamo, 2014). Occupiers facing homelessness are affected by higher rates of self-destructive actions such as substance abuse and suicides, anxiety, depression, high blood pressure, smoking, anger and violent behaviour towards others including family and mistreatment of children (Downing, 2016; Ross and Squires, 2011; Tsai, 2015; Vásquez-Vera et al., 2017).

During severe cold weather shocks, low-income UK households make choices between heat and eat (Beatty et al., 2014). In properties where rent is charged inclusive of fuel bills energy price increases have presented difficulties in recovering higher costs. These are potentially a trigger for illegal evictions. In cases where landlords do not pay fuel bills, utility companies have incorrectly pursued tenants for liability even when evicted for arrears (Lott-Lavignia, 2023; openDemocracy, 2023, Spencer and Rugg, 2023). Failure to ensure housing benefit payments keep pace with the cost of living in recent years left the poorest tenants in the private rented sector with the choice 'heat, eat or pay rent' struggling with a shortfall of up to £140 per week. The worst effects were found in London (Butler, 2018; Clarke et al., 2017).

The Trussell Trust (2023), who oversee 1,300 food banks across the UK, have reported a 37% increase in demand, the highest rate seen since the peak of the COVID-19 pandemic. Fifty-seven per cent of food bank users in receipt of Universal Credit experienced deductions and reported facing more than one day without any food or only eating one meal owing to the inability to afford sufficient food in the past month.

The government was urged to increase legal aid funding by a minimum of 15% to retain and recruit legal professionals and ensure resources remain in place for persons needing free legal advice (UK Parliament, 2023). The problem was made worse owing to delays in court procedures that arose during the COVID-19 pandemic. Since then, court backlogs have increased affecting public access to justice. Delays in court hearings are at a record high, in 2014, one in 20

Crown Court cases took longer than a year to be heard. The current figure is one in five (Quilter-Pinner and Khan, 2023) and highest in Crown Courts where illegal eviction cases are often heard (Richards and Davies, 2023). The pandemic merely exacerbated already existent problems caused by legal aid cuts made under the Legal Aid, Sentencing and Punishment of Offenders Act (2012). Cuts have prevented 'marginalised and vulnerable groups' from accessing legal aid support, most notably within economically deprived areas of London, the North West, Yorkshire and Humber (Bolt Burdon Kemp LLP, 2023; Makinson, 2021).

Mortgage and landlord possession claims increased by 25% across England and Wales during January to March 2023, the highest it has been since the same period of 2020 (Ministry of Justice, 2023). In 2019, small claims courts processing rental arrears and tenants' compensation claims took approximately 37 weeks to be heard this has now increased to an average of 51.9 weeks.

In Tribunals where rent repayment order cases or appeals against local authority enforcement measures are heard, there was an increase from 30 weeks in 2019 to 45 weeks in 2021 (HM Courts & Tribunal Service, 2023). Post-pandemic the growth of ineffective cases being brought before the courts is a worrying trend leading to greater inefficiencies because lawyers spend time and resources preparing cases that never proceed and court spaces are not used to full capacity (Richards and Davies, 2023).

The situation had an unintended effect on the abolition of Section 21. Ahead of the second reading of the Renters (Reform) Bill, it was announced that abolition of Section 21 is paused whilst the government works with the courts and MOJ to reform their systems capacity to process possession claims prioritising cases of rent arrears and anti-social behaviour, particularly complex cases (Levelling Up, Housing and Communities Committee, 2023). Whilst reformation is welcomed, tenant support groups believe it should not have been prioritised by delaying Section 21's removal because the ongoing situation inflicts continual disruption upon vulnerable tenants increasing homeless cases and insecurity of tenure through no fault of their own (Citizens Advice Newcastle and Gateshead, 2023; Crisis, 2023; Shelter, 2023).

Whilst tenant groups believe Section 21 evictions are unfair, landlord representatives have reported to the APPG-PRS (2023) that the eviction amendments to the Renters (Reform) Bill following Section 21 abolition would only have worked if courts can efficiently process possession claims. But court reformations have been ongoing for at least seven years under a program costing £1.3 billion. The committee are concerned the project is behind schedule and unable to sufficiently reduce 'extensive backlogs'. The completion timetable was continually extended and is currently set for March 2025 (HM Courts & Tribunals Service, 2024). This deadline is disputed by Quilter-Pinner and Khan (2023), who believe even with sufficient reformatory measures the backlog will take at least a decade to clear. This is discussed further in the chapter on feasibility.

The government tried to make all tenancies periodic under the now defunct Renters (Reform) Bill to allow flexibility for both tenants and landlords (DLUHC, 2022, 2023a). In this, iteration tenants could move, giving two months' notice, allowing landlords sufficient warning to avoid empty periods minimising rental losses during the vacancy. Provision of written agreement and terms were to be mandatory ensuring understanding on both sides (DLUHC, 2023a; Wilson and Cromarty, 2023). Theoretically, a tenant could have given two months' notice to quit on the same day they collected keys unintentionally impacting upon rental collection and agency fee models, consequently becoming mutually disadvantageous to tenants and landlords' long-term security (Propertymark, 2023; Smith, 2023). LARG (2023) wanted to restrict tenants' ability to use this clause for the first four months of occupancy to ensure the security of tenure will last more than two months.

Registered providers of student accommodation were proposed to be exempt from issuing periodic tenancies, but private landlords renting to students would not have been (Wilson and Cromarty, 2023). The government felt this gave students flexibility to remain in properties after graduation. Landlords whose business model is to let to students raised concerns that student tenancies should be fixed-term and aligned with the academic year. The changes would have meant they cannot re-let to new students unless current tenants gave two months' notice, thus unintentionally decreasing available student accommodation. Concerns remained that fixed terms contracts could leave students in poorly maintained properties locked into agreements and unable to leave (Levelling Up, Housing and Communities Committee, 2023; Wilson and Cromarty, 2023). The government made a small concession to allow students on joint tenancies in shared HMO properties to be exempt from periodic tenancies, but this exemption would not have applied to students in smaller lettings or landlords who let room by room (Stewart et al., 2024).

None of the proposed grounds for possession contained in the now defunct Renters (Reform) Bill would have been able to be used by landlords if not previously set out in tenancy agreements. A landlord for example who is considering selling in future or giving the property to a relative would have to stipulate in the agreement possession may be sought under those grounds. Were a landlord to specify a ground for possession in an eviction notice without having first included the clause in the tenancy agreement, this would have invalidated the notice making the eviction illegal. Following a legitimate use of these eviction grounds either on the basis that the landlord or his family will move in, or the property was to be sold, provisions under the Renters (Reform) Bill would have prevented a property being re-let or marketed for three months. Landlords would also have been required to update the property's status on the new property portal (DLUHC, 2023a; Wilson and Cromarty, 2023). Citizens Advice (2023) and Shelter (APPG-PRS, 2023) raised concerns these grounds were open to abuse because landlords were not required to evidence – they are either selling the property or housing their family. Furthermore, a three-month void period seems a small price to pay for a landlord wishing to instigate retaliatory evictions under the guise of these provisions. Tenant support groups called for landlords to be required to produce a high threshold of evidence and for severe consequences for 'gaming the system' (ACORN, 2023; APPG-PRS, 2023; Citizens Advice Newcastle and Gatesehead, 2023). Furthermore, the application of this ground and instigation of periodic tenancies was criticised because currently tenants under an AST issued for 12 months enjoy comparatively longer periods with security of tenure (Citizens Advice, 2023).

There was also an amendment allowing mandatory possession where rent was paid even one day late (three times), over a three-year period (DLUHC, 2023b; Wilson and Cromarty, 2023), placing tenants in low-paid work in a vulnerable position particularly if experiencing income losses through unemployment, reduced hours or ill health, all issues with potential resolutions achieved through debt management (Crisis, 2023; HCCPA, 2022c; National Debtline, 2023; Peaker, 2023). At present, local authorities do not have statutory obligations to rehouse tenants evicted under Section 8 who could be classed as 'intentionally homeless', unless following the removal of Section 21, the prevention duty is then carried over to Section 8 (Crisis, 2023; openDemocracy, 2023; Shelter, 2023). National Debtline (2023) believed an exemption should be made to this clause for delays arising from benefits paid in arrears. According to Stewart et al. (2024), arrears arising from

Universal Credit payment delays were to be discounted from evictions for arrears exceeding two months.

A further concern was a proposed amendment to grounds for discretionary possession allowed on the basis that a tenant's behaviour was 'likely to cause' nuisance or annoyance. The proposal was to amend the definition so that possession can be sought on the basis that the tenant's behaviour is 'capable of causing' nuisance or annoyance (Cummins, 2023; DLUHC, 2023b; Smith, 2023; Wilson and Cromarty, 2023). The ambiguity of this proposed definition raised concerns the clause can potentially be misused (Local Government Association (LGA), 2023). A possible unintended effect of either of these elements could be that a disrepair complaint could lead to either of these grounds, i.e. mandatory possession for arrears or because the landlord feels the behaviour is 'capable of causing' nuisance being instigated to initiate a retaliatory eviction. Or simply these grounds being used as threats to discourage occupiers from complaining.

The idea of legislation to enable lead authority regulatory oversight over the private rented sector lacked clarity on how it will work (CIEH, 2023). Primary authority schemes were criticised because they regulate through contractual arrangements whereby large national food chains pay primary authorities to oversee regulation centrally with less oversight across national outlets. If a local authority wishes to prosecute, they can only do so with the primary authority's permission. There is potential for policy capture here because primary authorities are paid by the company and can block enforcement if they feel primary authority advice was followed. The food company can also refer the matter to the Office for Product and Safety Standards if they feel local enforcement conflicts with primary authority advice (Office for Product Safety Standards, 2017; Tombs, 2016). Primary authority schemes are expensive for lead authorities to maintain cost-effectively without adequate resourcing. The overarching duties of primary authority oversight are often prioritised at the opportunity cost of attending to the statutory duties within the authority's own area thus creating an inequality in service (CIEH, 2023).

For other civil financial penalties, the proposal to set penalties for breaches of requirements under the Renters (Reform) Bill initially up to £5,000 (Wilson and Cromarty, 2023) was seen as an ineffective deterrent, inconsistent with other financial penalty measures available under the Housng and Planning Act (2016) and the Leasehold Reform (Ground Rent) Act (2022). Both acts allow local authorities discretion to impose fines of up to £30,000. Apart from offences under the Protection from Eviction Act, the Renters (Reform) Bill would only have allowed fines of up to £30,000 for repeated or continuous offences.

Considering the legislative attempts to regulate the private rented sector, Spencer and Rugg (2023) acknowledge part of the reason why so many unintended effects persist is that successive governments never prioritised monitoring and collating data on the incidence rate of illegal evictions and harassment or considered developing an established means of measuring this data and learning from it before making any further legislative changes. Such measures could be used as a baseline or benchmark in future analysis of the impact of any new related legislation when passed into law and implemented.

Solutions to issues raised regarding practicalities of periodic tenancies will depend upon agreed lengths of time following tenancy uptake before clauses are used. Mandatory possession for three late rental payments is harsh, lending weight to perceptions landlords' interests were favoured over tenants without consideration for effects upon homeless prevention resources.

Increasing rental rates, high energy bills and low enforcement against illegal eviction expose tenants to physical or psychological health hazards, amidst cycles of poverty facing choices over low-incomes expenditure on rent, food and thermal comfort. Removing any of these gives rise to associated risk factors and health hazards. Knowledge of protections for eviction is poor amongst landlords, tenants, police and local authorities. Skill depletion has lowered protections allowing avoidable illegal or retaliatory evictions to proceed, but this will likely reduce if policymakers abolish Section 21 and the need for Deregulation Act protections. Levels of financial penalties for most offences under the Renters (Reform) Bill would have been insufficient to deter non-compliance. Any future policy reformation of the private rented sector will need to be mindful that complexities arising from subsequent amendments to other eviction procedures could deter usage and see more landlords resort to illegal eviction.

References

ACORN. (2023, November). Written Evidence. House of Commons Public Bill Committee. Renters (Reform) Bill. RRB24.

APPG for the Private Rented Sector. (2023, December). *Ensuring Rental Reform Works for Tenants and Landlords. A Vision for the Private Rented Sector of the Future*. Propertymark. Available from: https://www.propertymark.co.uk/static/fe6fd918-c274-405f-813539a518191797/Ensuring-Rental-Reform-Works-for-Tenants-and-Landlords.pdf

Battersby, S. and Pointing, J. (2019). Statutory Nuisance and Residential Property: Environmental Health Problems in Housing. Abingdon, Oxon: Routledge.

Beatty, T.K.M., Blow, L. and Crossley, T.F. (2014). 'Is There a "Heat-or-Eat" Trade-Off in the UK?', *Journal of the Royal Statistical Society. Series A, Statistics in Society*, 177(1), pp. 281–294.

Böheim, R. and Taylor, M.P. (2000). 'My Home was My Castle: Evictions and Repossessions in Britain', *Journal of Housing Economics*, 9, pp. 287–319.

Bolt Burdon Kemp LLP. (2023). *Inequality within Britain's Legal Aid Funding System*. [online]. Available from: https://www.bolt burdonkemp.co.uk/our-insights/campaigns/inequality-in-britains-legal-aid-funding-system/

Butler, P. (2018) 'Low-Income Tenants Face "Heat, Eat or Pay Rent" Choices; Housing Benefit Freeze Leaving Poorest Private Renters with Shortfall of up to 140 a Week', *The Guardian*, 29 August.

Chartered Institute of Environmental Health (CIEH). (2023, November). Written Evidence. House of Commons Public Bill Committee. Renters (Reform) Bill. RRB50.

Citizens Advice. (2023, June 15). 'An End to Unfair Evictions?', *citizensadvice.org.uk*. [online]. Available from: https://www.citizen sadvice.org.uk/about-us/our-work/policy/policy-research-topics/housing-policy-research/an-end-to-unfair-evictions/

Citizens Advice Newcastle and Gatesehead. (2023, November). Written Evidence. House of Commons Public Bill Committee. Renters (Reform) Bill. RRB41.

Clarke, A., Hamilton, C., Jones, M. and Muir, K. (2017). *Poverty, Evictions and Forced Moves*. Joseph Rowntree Foundation. (July 2017, updated 3 August 2017).

Clarke, D. (2020, June 3). *An Uncivil Matter: Unlawful Eviction and the Police*. Doughty Street Chambers. [online]. Available from: https://insights.doughtystreet.co.uk/post/102g8qi/an-uncivil-matter-unlawful-eviction-and-the-police

Communities and Local Government Committee. (2013, January). Written Evidence Submitted by the Association of Tenancy Relations Officers. Commons Select Committees.

Community Law Partnership. (2018, June 25). 'Review of the Legal Aid, Sentencing and Punishment of Offenders Act 2012. ("LASPOA")', *communitylawpartnership.co.uk*. [online]. Available from: https://www.communitylawpartnership.co.uk/news/review-of-the-legal-aid-sentencing-and-punishment-of-offenders-act-2012-laspoa

Crisis. (2023, November). Written Evidence. House of Commons Public Bill Committee. Renters (Reform) Bill. RRB21.

Cummins, S. (2023, June 28). *Renters (Reform) Bill: Key Provisions, Implications For Landlords & Tenants*. Anthony Gold Solicitors.

[online]. Available from: https://anthonygold.co.uk/latest/blog/renters-reform-bill

Department for Communities and Local Government. (2012, August). *Evidence Review of the Costs of Homelessness*. London: DCLG.

Department for Levelling Up, Housing and Communities. (2022, May 11). *Government to Deliver 'New Deal' for Renters*. London: DLUHC.

Department for Levelling Up, Housing and Communities. (2023a, May 12). *Renters (Reform) Bill Impact Assessment. DLUHC 2564*. London: DLUHC.

Department for Levelling Up, Housing and Communities. (2023b, May 17). 'Guide to the Renters (Reform) Bill', *GOV.UK*. [online]. Available from: https://www.gov.uk/guidance/guide-to-the-renters-reform-bill

Deregulation Act 2015 c.20. Available from: https://www.legislation.gov.uk/ukpga/2015/20/contents/enacted

Desmond, M. (2012). 'Eviction and the Reproduction of Urban Poverty', *The American Journal of Sociology*, 118, pp. 88–133.

Desmond, M. and Kimbro, R.T. (2015). 'Eviction's Fallout: Housing, Hardship, and Health', *Social Forces*, 94(1), pp. 295–324.

Downing, J. (2016) 'The Health Effects of the Foreclosure Crisis and Unaffordable Housing: A Systematic Review and Explanation of Evidence', *Social Science & Medicine (1982)*, 162, pp. 88–96.

Enwerem v Montague and Delucter Ltd and Bility. (2023). LON/00AL/HMK/2022/0007.

HM Courts & Tribunal Service. (2023, December 14). HMCTS Management Information – Reformed Services September 2023. Available from: https://www.gov.uk/government/statistical-data-sets/hmcts-management-information-reformed-services-september-2023

HM Courts & Tribunals Service. (2024, February 23). The HMCTS Reform Programme. Available from: https://www.gov.uk/guidance/the-hmcts-reform-programme

House of Commons Committee of Public Accounts. (2022a, January). Written Evidence Submitted by Transparency International UK. PRP0007.

House of Commons Committee of Public Accounts. (2022b, January). Written Evidence Submitted by ACORN. PRP0003.

House of Commons Committee of Public Accounts. (2022c, January). Written Evidence Submitted by StepChange Debt Charity. PRP0005.

House of Commons Committee of Public Accounts. (2022d, January). Written Evidence Submitted by Glass Door Homeless Charity. PRP0006.

Housing and Planning Act 2016 c.22. Available from: https://www.legislation.gov.uk/ukpga/2016/22/contents/enacted

Large Agents Representation Group (LARG). (2023, November). Written Evidence. House of Commons Public Bill Committee. Renters (Reform) Bill. RRB17.

Leasehold Reform (Ground Rent) Act 2022 c.1. Available from: https://www.legislation.gov.uk/ukpga/2022/1/contents/enacted

Legal Aid, Sentencing and Punishment of Offenders Act 2012 c.10. Available from: https://www.legislation.gov.uk/ukpga/2012/10/contents/enacted (accessed 22 October 2023).

Levelling Up, Housing and Communities Committee. (2023, October 20). *Reforming the Private Rented Sector: Government's Response to the Committee's Fifth Report of Session 2022–23: HC 1935.* London: House of Commons.

Local Government Association. (2023, November 7). 'Renters' Reform Bill, Committee Stage, House of Commons', *local.gov.uk.* Available from: https://www.local.gov.uk/parliament/briefings-and-responses/renters-reform-bill-committee-stage-house-commons-7-november

Lott-Lavignia, R. (2023, March 16). 'Vulnerable renters 'hounded' by utility companies to pay off landlord debts', *openDemcracy.* Available from: https://www.opendemocracy.net/en/vulnerable-tenants-edf-energy-thames-water-landlord-bills/

Makinson, R. (2021, August 26). 'LASPO: How A Near-Decade of Legal Aid Cuts Has Affected Britain's Most Vulnerable', *Lawyer Monthly.* [online]. Available from: https://www.lawyer-monthly.com/2021/08/laspo-how-a-near-decade-of-legal-aid-cuts-has-affected-britains-most-vulnerable/

Marsh, A., Forrest, R., Kennett, P., Niner, P. and Cowan, D. (2000). *Harassment and Unlawful Eviction of Private Rented Sector Tenants and Park Home Residents.* Department of Environment, Transport and the Regions. University of Bristol Law School.

Ministry of Housing Communities and Local Government. (2018). *Overcoming the Barriers to Longer Tenancies in the Private Rented Sector.* London: MHCLG. (updated 15 April 2019).

Ministry of Housing Communities and Local Government. (2019, January). *English Private Landlord Survey 2018.* London: MHCLG.

Ministry of Housing, Communities and Local Government. (2020/2021, July 8). *English Housing Survey 2019 to 2020. Annex Tables 3.7 and 3.11.* London: MHCLG.

Ministry of Justice. (2023, June 1). National Statistics. Civil Justice Statistics Quarterly: January to March 2023.

Moore, H. (2023, November 20). 'The Families Stuck Living in Britain's Unlicensed Bedsits', *Today in Focus, Podcast* Available from: https://www.theguardian.com/uk-news/audio/2023/nov/20/the-families-stuck-living-in-britains-unlicensed-bedsits-podcast

Morestin, F. (2012, September 2012). *A Framework for Analyzing Public Policies: Practical Guide*. National Collaborating Centre for Healthy Public Policy. [online]. Available from: http://www.ncchpp. ca/docs/Guide_framework_analyzing_policies_En.pdf

National Audit Office. (2019). *Written Evidence Submitted by the National Audit Office: FSR 112*. London: UK Parliament.

National Debtline (2023, November). Written Evidence. House of Commons Public Bill Committee. Renters (Reform) Bill. RRB23.

Office for Product Safety Standards. (2017). *Primary Authority: A Guide for Businesses*. (updated 11 May 2018). Available from: https:// www.gov.uk/guidance/primary-authority-a-guide-for-businesses

openDemocracy. (2023, November). Written Evidence. House of Commons Public Bill Committee. Renters (Reform) Bill. RRB48.

Peaker, G. (2023, May 17). 'Renters (Reform) Bill – the Good, the Potentially Good and the Ugly. Part 1', *Nearly Legal*. [online]. Available from: https://nearlylegal.co.uk/2023/05/renters-reform-bill-the-good-the-potentially-good-and-the-ugly-part-1/

Propertymark. (2023, November). Written Evidence. House of Commons Public Bill Committee. Renters (Reform) Bill. RRB48.

Protection from Eviction Act 1977 c.43. Available from: https://www. legislation.gov.uk/ukpga/1977/43 (accessed 22 October 2023).

Quilter-Pinner, H. and Khan, H. (2023, December). *Great Government Public Service Reform in the 2020s*. London: Institute for Public Policy Research.

Reeve, K., Bimpson, E., Batty, E., Chambers, J., Goodchild, B., McCarthy, L., Redman, J., Sanderson, E., Speake, B. and Wilson, I. (2022, June 16). *Local Authority Enforcement in the Private Rented Sector: Headline Report. Department for Levelling Up*. London: Housing and Communities.

Reeve-Lewis, B., Bolton, J.L. and Rugg, J. (2022, May). *Offences Under the Protection from Eviction Act 1977 in England and Wales: A Report from Safer Renting*. London: Safer Renting. Cambridge House.

Reis, S. (2019). *A Home of Her Own, Housing and Women*. Womens' Budget Group. [online]. Available from: https://wbg.org.uk/analysis/ reports/a-home-of-her-own-housing-and-women/

Richards, G. and Davies, N. (2023, October 30). *Performance Tracker 2023: Criminal Courts*. Institute for Government. Available from: https://www.instituteforgovernment.org.uk/publication/ performance-tracker-2023/criminal-courts

Ross, L.M. and Squires, G.D. (2011, February, 3). 'The Personal Costs of Subprime Lending and the Foreclosure Crisis: A Matter of Trust, Insecurity, and Institutional Deception'. *Social Science Quarterly. Together*, 92(1), pp. 140–163.

Rugg, J. and Wallace, A. (2021). *Property Supply to the Lower End of the English Private Rented Sector*. New York: Centre for Housing Policy, University of York.

Sagoe, C., Ehrlich, R., Reynolds, L. and Rich, H. (2020). *Time for Change: Marking Renting Fairer for Private Landlords*. London: Shelter.

Shelter. (2022, June 10). 'Revenge Eviction If You Ask for Repairs', *england.shelter.org*. [online]. Available from: https://england.shelter.org.uk/housing_advice/repairs/revenge_eviction_if_you_ask_for_repairs

Shelter. (2023, November). Written Evidence. House of Commons Public Bill Committee. Renters (Reform) Bill. RRB09.

Smith, D. (2023, May 17). *Renters' Reform Finally Arrives*. JMW Solicitors LLP. [online]. Available from: https://www.jmw.co.uk/blog/commercial-litigation-dispute-resolution/renters-reform-finally-arrives

Spencer, R., Reeve-Lewis, B., Rugg, J. and Barata, E. (2020) 'Journeys in the Shadow Private Rented Sector', Cambridge House/Centre for Housing Policy, 47.

Spencer, R. and Rugg, J. (2023, November). *Offences Under the Protection from Eviction Act 1977 in England- 2022 Update of the Annual Count, Safer Renting*. Available from: https://ch1889.org/wp-content/uploads/2023/12/PfEA-2022-offences-count-Safer-Renting-11-2023.pdf

Stewart, R., Basin, N. and Saeed, R. (2024). 'Housing Law Reform Webinar – Planning for life after the Renters (Reform) Act', *Anthony Gold*. Available from: https://anthonygold.co.uk/agevents/renters-reform-bill

Tombs, S. (2016, April 14). *'Better Regulation': Better for Whom?* London: Centre for Crime and Justice Studies. Available from: https://www.crimeandjustice.org.uk/sites/crimeandjustice.org.uk/files/Better%20regulation%20briefing%2C%20April%202016_0.pdf

Trussell Trust. (2023). *Emergency Food Parcel Distribution in the UK: April 2022 – March 2023*. [online]. Available from: https://www.trusselltrust.org/wp-content/uploads/sites/2/2023/04/EYS-UK-Factsheet-2022-23.pdf

Tsai, A. (2015). 'Home Foreclosure, Health, and Mental Health: A Systematic Review of Individual, Aggregate, and Contextual Associations', *PLoS One*, 10, p. e0123182. Available from: https://doi.org/10.1371/journal.pone.0123182

Tsai, J. and Huang, M. (2019). 'Systematic Review of Psychosocial Factors Associated with Evictions', *Health & Social Care in the Community*, 27(3), pp. e1–e9. Available from: https://doi.org/10.1111/hsc.12619

Tsai, J., Jones, N., Szymkowiak, D. and Rosenheck, R.A. (2020) 'Longitudinal Study of the Housing and Mental Health Outcomes of Tenants Appearing in Eviction Court', *Social Psychiatry and Psychiatric Epidemiology*, 56(9), pp. 1679–1686.

Turunen, E. and Hiilamo, H. (2014). 'Health Effects of Indebtedness: A Systematic Review', *BMC Public Health*, 14, p. 489. [online]. Available from: https://doi.org/10.1186/1471-2458-14-489

UK Parliament. (2023). *The Future of Legal Aid.* House of Commons. [online]. Available from: https://committees.parliament.uk/work/531/the-future-of-legal-aid/

Vásquez-Vera, H., Palència, L., Magna, I., Mena, C., Neira, J. and Borrell, C. (2017). 'The Threat of Home Eviction and Its Effects on Health Through the Equity Lens: A Systematic Review', *Social Science & Medicine*, 175, pp. 199–208.

Wilson, W. (2023, October 30). *Can Private Landlords Refuse to Let to Benefit Claimants and People with Children?* London: House of Commons Library.

Wilson, W., Barton, C. and Cromarty, H. (2022, October 24). *The End of 'No Fault' Section 21 Evictions (England).* London: House of Commons Library Research Briefing.

Wilson, W. and Cromarty, H. (2023, October 21). *Research Briefing: Renters (Reform) Bill 2022–23: CBP08756.* London: House of Commons Library.

5 Housing Policy, Social Inequalities and Equitability

The relevant housing policies are further examined in this chapter to determine what the intended or unintended effects are on different groups categorised by gender, socioeconomic status, family or single status, drink or drug dependency, ethnicity and private renting. The purpose of analysing equity is to determine whether policy implementation creates or reinforces social inequalities in health, or whether there is a potential to create, increase or correct these inequalities. Morestin (2012) explains this is important because whilst a policy may show improvements at the population level, there is a danger that it can simultaneously 'deepen social inequalities'.

Amidst concerns about poor administration of Local Housing Allowance and increasing rates of homelessness and housing demand, the Communities and Local Government Select Committee (CLGSC) (2016) conducted an inquiry to determine whether Local Housing Allowance procedures were a causal factor in homelessness. Tenants receiving local housing allowance do not have the choice of whether to receive payments directly or for payment to go directly to landlords. Many claimants prefer paying landlords directly for better financial management. The intention behind paying tenants directly was to give them more choice over where to rent and promote greater responsibility, but lack of choice over how the allowance is paid has undermined this purpose (Albanese and Baxendale, 2009; Reeve et al., 2016; Wilson, 2023).

The CLGSC (2016) recommended more flexibility in payment methods to restore landlord's confidence and reduce occupiers' risk of eviction for rental arrears. The inquiry also took account of a report from Sheffield Hallam University on behalf of Crisis (Reeve et al., 2016) finding 55% of landlords unwilling to let to tenants on housing benefits and 82% of landlords reluctant to let to homeless

DOI: 10.1201/9781032705071-5

households. Amongst the few willing to let to households classed as homeless many were allocating fewer properties within their portfolio for these purposes, 75% allocated less than 10% of their housing stock for homeless households (CLGSC, 2016; Reeve et al., 2016; Wilson, 2023). More recently the English Private Landlord Survey 2021–2022 reported one in ten private renters (109,000 households) had during the previous year experienced refusal of a tenancy because they receive benefits (DLUHC, 2022a).

Reluctance amongst landlords to let to tenants on benefits stems from the time it takes to process applications and for rent to be paid (Wilson, 2023). A greater acceptance exists amongst landlords of tenants on benefits in areas where the market has larger numbers of tenants in receipt of benefits compared to prospective tenants who are non-recipients. In areas of higher demand where landlords have more choice, there is a greater incentive to rent to tenants who are not benefit-dependent and more unwillingness to let to those that are (Beatty et al., 2013; Wilson, 2023).

The government's impact assessment on the Renters (Reform) Bill notes that asymmetry of information regarding a property is in the landlord's favour. In a housing market where demand outstrips supply, this allows landlords to be price setters. The unscrupulous amongst them can take advantage in this market, setting rent at inflated prices (DLUHC, 2023a).

Furthermore, the effects of high rents and insufficient coverage through Local Housing Allowance or Universal Credit place vulnerable tenants unintentionally at risk of eviction (HCCPA, 2022a, 2022b; Wilson, 2023). When compared to the average level of private rents in an area, an inquiry by the Work and Pensions Select Committee (2014) noted that the 'growing discrepancy' between rents and claimable allowances increases the risk of homelessness through eviction for arrears or non-renewal of tenancies, often the difference was sufficient to cause concern that allowances fail to fully cover rent leading to arrears (DLUHC, 2022c; Wilson, 2023; Work and Pensions Select Committee, 2014). This is explored further in the chapter on costs.

In London, the rate of possession orders is more than double the rest of England (Aldridge et al., 2015) and landlords easily impose rental increases without maintaining property conditions (Hafford-Letchfield et al., 2019). Where properties remain affordable under local housing allowance, the Work and Pensions Select Committee (2014) observed accommodation is often of poorer quality. Furthermore, many households are now trapped in the sector excluded from home ownership through lack of affordability, where once renting was considered a stepping stone from tenancy to ownership (Coulter, 2017).

Often securing private rented accommodation means tenants must move away from relatives and established communities and support mechanisms. For vulnerable adults, loss of support contributes to the breakdown of tenancies, particularly for tenants with substance dependencies or mental health issues or adjusting to life following a period of incarceration. This also presents challenges for support workers tasked with putting strategies in place to support the effective management of these tenancies (Ellison et al., 2012; Hafford-Letchfield et al., 2019).

Tenant family households also worry that moving will disrupt their children's education because eviction does not always align with school terms. Children of tenants lacking secure tenure experience worse educational outcomes through less engagement from teachers and disruption of friendships (Centre for Social Justice, 2021; Children's Society, 2020). Frequent churn of tenure in the private rented sector is argued to be detrimental to neighbourhood safety, wellbeing and productivity (Centre for Social Justice, 2021).

In a survey of 9,000 landlords with registered tenancy deposits, 44% confirmed they would not let to tenants on benefits. Eighty-four per cent of landlords when surveyed in 2022 said they would not want to let to tenants with a history of arrears (DLUHC, 2022b). There has been a growing rise in the practice of some landlords and agents specifying 'no DSS' or 'no kids' on letting adverts (Wilson, 2023) raising criticisms of indirect discrimination because income and employments status are not protected characteristics under the Equality Act 2010 (NAO, 2021; Wilson, 2023). The counter-argument is that indirect discrimination can be lawful if it is a proportionate method to achieve legitimate aims. According to Peaker (2020), a landlord with a mortgage agreement with a clause against letting to tenants on benefits could raise this as a justification. Such restrictions are perceived as a risk by landlords (Wilson, 2023). In oral evidence given by Shelter at the House of Commons, this argument was rejected because Section 142 of the Equality Act 2010 renders a contract unenforceable where an effect of a clause results in unlawful discrimination and there are no mortgage or insurance restrictions in letting to families with children (Work and Pensions Committee, 2019; Wilson, 2023).

In July 2020, a case heard at York County Court where Shelter's strategic litigation team represented a disabled single parent on housing benefit who had experienced a rejection of their tenancy application owing to these circumstances was ruled by the court as being indirectly discriminatory on sex and disability grounds, both defined characteristics under the Equality Act 2010 and therefore unlawful (Nearly Legal, 2020; Shelter, 2020). The judge noted over 53.1% of female single-parent households are in receipt of the benefit compared to 34% of male single households. If couples are considered, then 18.8% of women who are private tenants claim benefits compared to 12.4% of men. The judge concluded women are 1.5 times more likely to experience exclusion from the private rented sector through a blanket 'no DSS' ban than men (Wilson, 2023). In 2023, the Property Ombudsman ruled in another case taken by Shelter's strategic litigation team that a 'no kids' specification breaches the Ombudsman's code of practice and is disadvantageous towards women (Shelter, 2023; Wilson, 2023).

The effect of the legal ruling in July 2020 and later cases may have put a stop to 'No kids' appearing in adverts, but this can be subverted through affordability checks (Wilson, 2023). In a survey of private renters in England conducted in 2022, a disproportionate number of respondents with families (627) were refused tenancies by landlords unwilling to rent to families with children, the data was weighted with EHS data estimating that the number of English households affected by this discriminatory practice was 289,506 (Shelter, 2023; Wilson, 2023). Where tenants on benefits are excluded from available accommodation, they are unable to exercise choice and are ripe for exploitation. Often tenants on low incomes have English as a second language, are unfamiliar with their rights and are susceptible to placement in poor accommodation where multiple housing and tenancy offences proliferate and criminal landlords maximise profit (Spencer et al., 2020).

From 1991 to 2011, disproportionate numbers of ethnic minorities across England and Wales were housed in properties with poor conditions experiencing higher proportions of overcrowding compared with White British residents across districts with both small and large minority populations and high and low deprivation levels (Finney et al., 2016; Ratcliffe, 2002,). Outside London, disproportionate numbers of Pakistani or Bangladeshi households are concentrated within pre-1919 terraced housing. The 1991 census data showed overcrowding was prevalent amongst these groups and intense grouping also segregates them from the wider community much more so than for black household renters who are mainly social housing tenants (Ratcliffe, 2002). The EHS of 2020–2021 estimated 759,000 households (17% of private renters) mainly couples with young children were dissatisfied with their properties, 37% have damp and condensation issues and one in seven live in overcrowded conditions and 22% of tenants had moved not out of choice in the past 12 months (DLUHC, 2021, 2022b).

The resolve amongst tenants towards the degree of disrepair considered tolerable is variable (CLGC, 2013). According to the NAO (2021), approximately 22% of rental households surveyed had backed down from complaining and 14% feared retaliatory eviction. Worries over the insecurity of tenure affected health, relationships, and ability to find work (HCCPA, 2022b). Tenants' circumstances vary as do their prospects of being rehoused. The difference between a tenant deciding to make an official complaint or staying silent is predetermined by weighing this all up (CLGC, 2013).

Whilst Data can be used to target policy initiatives to address housing inequalities (Finney et al., 2016), financial constraints restrict local authorities from taking proactive measures. Local authorities adopt responsive policies for housing complaints strongly reliant upon tenants to be aware of their rights and report problems. Where a complaint of disrepair is raised to the local council and where tenants subsequently vacate, there is unlikely to be any follow-up enforcement action particularly where there is lack of clarity around the owner's future intentions for the property (CLGC, 2013; NAO, 2021).

'Right to Rent' legislation that places responsibility upon Landlords to check whether prospective tenants with EU, EEA and Swiss citizenship are allowed to rent in the UK has exacerbated racial discrimination within the private rented sector excluding migrants or persons perceived as migrants or 'British people of colour' who don't possess passports from renting (HCCPA, 2022a; Sagoe et al., 2020). Eighty-seven per cent of agents surveyed in 2019 confirmed they are more likely to perform right-to-rent checks whilst landlords active for three or less years were more likely to carry out right-to-rent checks (66%) compared to 60% of landlords active between 4 and 10 years or 60% with 11 or more years' experience (MHCLG, 2020). According to Glassdoor, 25% of landlords surveyed showed reluctance to let to non-UK passport holders. The MHCLG found that 25% of landlords and 10% of agents also refused to let to these groups without giving reasons (HCCPA, 2022a; MHCLG, 2020).

When surveyed in 2018 for their views on longer tenancies, 36% of tenants were unaware that under the current system, they can request longer tenancies. Eighty-one per cent would accept these if offered for greater security of tenure, only 21% of those surveyed were in that position and the remainder having not been offered anything longer than 12 months. From this, the government infers tenants do not feel sufficiently empowered to ask (MHCLG, 2018).

In global terms, the UK's global ranking for people's accessibility to civil justice has slipped from 13 to 20 (World Justice Project, 2022). Service cuts to legal aid have reduced eligibility to 27% of the population. When introduced in 1949, legal aid was available to 80% of the population. Today, 72% of legal aid service users are from Black, Asian, Minority Ethnic (BAME) backgrounds; between 2011 and 2020, the total number of legal aid providers fell by 34% across England and Wales from 4,257 to 2,810 (Bolt Burdon Kemp LLP, 2023). The Law Society (2023) now say that across England and Wales, 25.3 million people no longer have access to a local provider of Legal aid for housing cases. This means that people on low incomes do not have equitable access to legal advice they are lawfully entitled to.

Across England and Wales, 162 Magistrates courts were closed over the past decade leaving 161 functioning, a further 90 County Courts were also closed, further restricting tenants' access to justice (Madge, 2019; UK Parliament, 2023). In London, these closures affected 20 County and Magistrates courts (Madge, 2019; Spencer et al., 2020). With closures, there are also delays in court hearings, which can lead to a 'poorer quality of justice' as overtime people's recollection of events fades. Delays increase the likelihood that victims of serious crimes trying to process trauma will withdraw cases partly because such delays equate to a feeling that justice is being denied (Richards and Davies, 2023).

Tenants who have a poor understanding of their rights usually because English is a second language often acquiesce to landlords and engage less in government surveys than landlords (MHCLG, 2018; Reeve-Lewis et al., 2022; Spencer et al., 2020). The government acknowledges that survey responses on proposals to abolish Section 21 illustrate that tenants show poor awareness of their rights regarding eviction and the provisions of the Deregulation Act 2015 acknowledging more work is required to raise awareness (MHCLG, 2018). However, amongst community groups who to a greater or lesser extent influence policy-making processes, the absence of tenants' groups from an equitable access in formal meetings with ministers shaping housing policy is very noticeable (Marks and Whiffen, 2021). Superior and direct access to ministers is granted to developers, and the 'highly professionalised landlords and property lobby'. These groups employ professional lobbyists to influence policy outcomes in their interest at pre-consultation stage, raising the question as to whether consultations are perfunctory (HCCPA, 2022c; Marks and Whiffen, 2021). The lack of opportunities for access for private renters is attributed partly to the lack of resources amongst these groups which are underfunded, poorly staffed and lacking facilities, none of which is experienced by those organisations representing landlords, developers, planners and think tanks. The inequality is exacerbated by consultation documents being only made exclusively available to groups with higher access (HCCPA, 2022c).

The 2013 ATRO report to the CLCG predates any protections brought about under the Deregulation Act 2015. At the time, the ATRO urged the government to strengthen protections against retaliatory eviction because it deters tenants from complaining. Then (and still now) when a housing advisor takes a tenant complaint, they must advise tenants that their landlord could respond with retaliatory eviction. According to the ATRO, landlords are incentivised to use the Section 21 process because it's easier to find other tenants possibly more vulnerable and less likely to make a fuss (CLGC, 2013). Reeve-Lewis et al. (2022) point out that removing Section 21 and making eviction procedures more difficult threatens landlords' business models making the renting to occupiers on lower incomes a higher risk, thus reducing market availability for a vulnerable section of society where landlords anticipate difficulties with arrears and anti-social behaviour.

Awareness of legislative requirements amongst landlords was noticeably higher amongst those who only recently become landlords. Amongst the more experienced landlords, awareness was greater in those with larger portfolios and managing agents (MHCLG, 2018, 2019). Seventy-five per cent of landlords surveyed did not belong to any professional landlord organisation, whilst 22% were either current or lapsed members. Half were unaware of the legislative framework to protect tenants against retaliatory eviction under the Deregulation Act, 2015 (MHCLG, 2018).

Since 2015, landlords or letting agents were required to issue tenants with a copy of the government's 'How to rent' guide at the outset of the tenancy providing details of what entering a tenancy agreement entails, information about deposits, necessary paperwork and permitted fees. Forty-eight per cent of landlords surveyed in 2019 were not issuing this guidance, whilst 83% of agents confirmed they were. The 52% of landlords who issue the guidance were mostly landlords with larger portfolios (68% of total landlords surveyed). Broadly the pattern bears similarity to right-to-rent checks in that landlords active for three or less years were more likely to issue the booklet (57%) compared to 45% of landlords active between 4 and 10 years or 50% with 11 or more years' experience (MHCLG, 2019).

The exemptions to the Homes (Fitness for Human Habitation) Act 2018 Section 1(2) are that landlords cannot be liable when tenants cause damage. Exemptions apply if remedial work requires permission from a superior landlord or third party but is refused. In bringing a case forward, the tenant must provide evidence and write a 'letter of claim' to the landlord notifying them of any defects at the earliest opportunity affording landlords a chance to respond and rectify within 20 days. Failure of landlords to respond either directly or via solicitors within the timescale is a breach of protocol. The response must include clarification on whether they admit liability or dispute it and include proposed actions or evidence of trying to address the problems or offers of compensation (DLUHC, 2019; MOJ, 2021).

Tenants wishing to make complaints can apply for legal aid to fight the case once a dispute resolution process has been exhausted and obtain a date for a court hearing. If successful, the court can order the landlord to carry out works to comply with Section 9(a) of the Landlord and Tenant Act 1985 making the property fit for human habitation for the remaining life of the lease and award damages to the tenant, (DLUHC, 2019).

Spencer et al. (2020) found law advisors and housing enforcers had low confidence in police support because of the poor understanding shown by police officers of how housing offences fit as a component of serious crime. Either police were believed to be poorly equipped or unwilling to act. Norfolk Constabulary (2019) responded to a freedom of information request to provide details on the numbers of unlawful eviction and harassment investigations carried out over the past decade disclosing six cases of unlawful eviction, two of which were poorly recorded, whilst the others were dropped through lack of evidence or withdrawal by the suspect or because the case was not deemed to be in the public interest. In the past decade, there was only one harassment case where the victim refused to identify the offender. According to

Spencer et al. (2020), the experience of occupiers was that they felt the police failed to support them even when landlords had stolen property or physically threatened them.

Enwerem *v* Montague and Delucter Ltd and Bility (2023) is a recent rent repayment order case heard at the First-tier tribunal concerning a pregnant tenant facing eviction. At the hearing, the applicant reported suffering from anxiety, high blood pressure and sleep disorder and gave birth via emergency caesarean. The tenant, her seven-year-old daughter and new-born infant found themselves locked out of the home one cold November afternoon. Eventually, she called the police for assistance only to be told that this was a civil matter; however, police did attend but refused to assist the tenant with gaining access even though her baby was crying 'uncontrollably' and her daughter was 'freezing'. The tenant was told by an officer that she could be arrested, and her children taken into care if she attempted entry. The tribunal recognised the police were concerned about a potential breach of the peace but were incorrect, effectively aiding and abetting an illegal eviction – a behaviour the tribunal acknowledged is not untypical in these cases. The landlord was present, and their version of events was taken by police at face value. The tribunal found in favour of the occupier and a repayment order was made for £5,400.

Norfolk Constabulary (2019) confirmed there is no specific training or guidance material provided to officers concerning harassment and eviction. Officers can refer to the Police Visual Handbook which contains extensive information on investigation and operational procedures and is available for officers electronically on laptops or smartphones (Police Community, 2012).

The Police Visual Handbook covers officers' powers of arrest as detailed under the Police and Criminal Evidence Act 1984 (PACE). According to Clarke (2020), Section 24 of PACE allows officers to arrest without warrant any person about to commit an offence or has committed an offence or is in the act of committing an offence for a set of specified reasons under Section 24(5). Of relevance here is that arrests can be made to prevent perpetrators from causing physical injury and to protect children or vulnerable persons. This means, according to Clarke, police can prosecute landlords for illegal eviction and harassment and arrest them during their investigations. Common law and Section 3 of the Criminal Law Act 1967 entitles police officers to use 'force as is reasonable in the circumstances in the prevention of crime'. This taken together with article 8 of the Human Rights Act 1988 would prompt courts to interpret these provisions as being compatible with the rights of the occupier and respect for private and family life. Tenants failed by the police during unlawful evictions may be able to claim against them for damages under the provisions of Section 7 of the Human Rights Act 1988 or challenge their actions through judicial review.

In August 2023, it was announced that the Metropolitan Police together with the GLA, Safer Renting and Generation Rent updated their training and guidance for police officers (Warren, 2023). Shelter (2023) provided a link on their website to downloadable forms with information for the police in attendance of an illegal eviction. It has a series of escalating actions beginning with a warning to the landlord that their actions may be illegal and to persuade them to desist and allow tenants to access the property. It also advises that police officers in this situation should gather evidence of any potential criminality such as harassment or breaches of the peace whilst at the scene. It also states that an arrest of the landlord or agent under Section 24(1) of the PACE 1984 could include circumstances where a landlord is attempting to force entry against the occupiers' wishes. Whilst this policy is London-centric and advises that a landlord should be reported to the London Assembly, it also states that outside London, officers should report to local private sector housing teams or tenancy relations officers, or the local homeless team if the tenant cannot regain access. There is no information as to whether this guidance has been incorporated into the Police Visual Handbook.

References

Albanese, F. and Baxendale, A. (2009, October). *Local Housing Allowance and Direct Payment – Giving Claimants a Choice*. England, London: Shelter.

Aldridge, H., Born, T.B., Tinson, A. and MacInnes, T. (2015, August). *London's Poverty Profile*. London: Trust for London and New Policy Institute.

Beatty, C., Cole, I., Powell, R., Crisp, R., Brewer, M., Browne, J., Emerson, C., Joyce, R., Kemp, P. and Pereira, I. (2013). *Monitoring the Impact of Changes to the Local Housing Allowance System of Housing Benefit, Interim Report – Summary, 2013*. London: Department for Work and Pensions.

Bolt Burdon Kemp LLP. (2023). *Inequality within Britain's Legal Aid Funding System.* [online]. Available from: https://www.bolt burdonkemp.co.uk/our-insights/campaigns/inequality-in-britains-legal-aid-funding-system/

Centre for Social Justice. (2021, June). *Pillars of Community. Why Communities Matter and What Matters to Them.* Westminster. [online]. Available from: https://www.centreforsocialjustice.org.uk/wp-content/uploads/2021/06/Pillars-of-Community.pdf

Children's Society. (2020). *Moving, Always Moving: The Normalisation of Housing Insecurity Among Children in Low Income Households in England.* [online]. Available from: https://www.child renssociety.org.uk/sites/default/files/2020-10/Moving-Always-Moving-Report.pdf

Clarke, D. (2020). An uncivil matter: Unlawful eviction and the police. (3 June 2020). *Doughty Street Chambers.* [online]. Available from: https://insights.doughtystreet.co.uk/post/102g8qi/an-uncivil-matter-unlawful-eviction-and-the-police

Communities and Local Government Committee. (2013, January). *Written Evidence Submitted by the Association of Tenancy Relations Officers.* Commons Select Committees. [online]. Available from: https://publications.parliament.uk/pa/cm201314/cmselect/cmcomloc/50/50iii94.htm

Communities and Local Government Select Committee. (2016, August 18). *Homelessness. Third Report of Session 2016–17: HC 40.* London: House of Commons.

Coulter, R. (2017). 'Local House Prices, Parental Background and Young Adults' Homeownership in England and Wales', *Urban Studies,* 54(14), pp. 3360–3379.

Department for Levelling Up, Housing & Communities. (2019). Guide for tenants: Homes (Fitness for Human Habitation) Act 2018. (6 March 2019). GOV.UK. [online]. Available from: https://www.gov.uk/government/publications/homes-fitness-for-human-habitation-act-2018/guide-for-tenants-homes-fitness-for-human-habitation-act-2018

Department for Levelling Up, Housing and Communities. (2021). *English Housing Survey 2020 to 2021: Headline Report.* London: DLUHC.

Department for Levelling Up, Housing and Communities. (2022a, December). *English Housing Survey Headline Report 2021–22.* London: DLUHC.

Department for Levelling Up, Housing and Communities. (2022b, May 11). *Government to Deliver 'New Deal' for Renters.* London: DLUHC.

Department for Levelling Up, Housing and Communities. (2022c, May 26). *English Private Landlord Survey 2021.* London: DLUHC.

Department for Levelling Up, Housing and Communities. (2023a, May 12). *Renters (Reform) Bill Impact Assessment: DLUHC 2564.* London: DLUHC.

Department for Levelling Up, Housing and Communities. (2023b, July 13). *English Housing Survey 2021 to 2022: Private Rented Sector.* London: DLUHC.

Ellison, A., Pleace, N. and Hanvey, E. (2012). *Meeting the Housing Needs of Vulnerable Homeless People in the Private Rented Sector in Northern Ireland. Housing Rights Service and Policies.* York: University of York.

Enwerem v Montague and Delucter Ltd and Bility. (2023). LON/00AL/HMK/2022/0007.

Equality Act 2010 c.15. Available from: https://www.legislation.gov.uk/ukpga/2010/15/contents (accessed 22 October 2023).

Finney, N., Lymperopolou, K., Kapoor, N., Marshall, A., Sabater, A. and Simpson, L. (2016). 'Local Ethnic Inequalities: Ethnic Differences in Education, Employment, Health and Housing in Districts of England and Wales, 2001–2011', *Social Policy and Practice*, 2, p. 57.

Hafford-Letchfield, T., Gleeson, H. and Mohammed, R. (2019) 'Vulnerable Adults in the Privately Rented Sector in England: A Snapshot of Current Practice Issues', *Practice (Birmingham, England)*, 31(2), pp. 97–115.

House of Commons Committee of Public Accounts. (2022a, January). Written Evidence Submitted by Glass Door Homeless Charity. PRP0006.

House of Commons Committee of Public Accounts. (2022b, January). Written Evidence Submitted by StepChange Debt Charity. PRP0005.

House of Commons Committee of Public Accounts. (2022c). Written evidence submitted by Transparency International UK. January 2022. PRP0007. [online]. UK Parliament. Written Evidence Regulation of Private Renting. Available from: https://committees.parliament.uk/writtenevidence/43018/pdf/

The Law Society. (2023, August 29). *Legal Aid Deserts.* Available from: https://www.lawsociety.org.uk/campaigns/civil-justice/legal-aid-deserts/

Madge, N. (2019). 'Selling Off Our Silver.' Legal Action Group. (July 2019). [online]. Available from: https://www.lag.org.uk/article/206681/selling-off-our-silver

Marks, T, Whiffen, R. (2021). House of Cards Exploring Access and Influence in UK Housing Policy. (July 2021). Transparency International UK. [online]. Available from: https://www.transparency.org.uk/sites/default/files/pdf/publications/House%20of%20Cards%20%20Transparency%20International%20UK%20%28web%29.pdf

Ministry of Housing Communities and Local Government. (2018). *Overcoming the Barriers to Longer Tenancies in the Private Rented Sector*. London: MHCLG. (updated 15 April 2019).

Ministry of Housing Communities and Local Government. (2019, January). *English Private Landlord Survey 2018*. London: MHCLG.

Ministry of Housing, Communities and Local Government. (2020/2021, July 8). *English Housing Survey 2019 to 2020. Annex Tables 3.7 and 3.11*. London: MHCLG.

Ministry of Justice. (2021). Pre-Action Protocol for Housing Conditions Claims (England). (19 August 2021). Justice.gov.uk. [online]. Available from: https://www.justice.gov.uk/courts/procedure-rules/civil/protocol/prot_hou

Morestin, F. (2012, September). *A Framework for Analyzing Public Policies: Practical Guide*. National Collaborating Centre for Healthy Public Policy. [online]. Available from: http://www.ncchpp.ca/docs/Guide_framework_analyzing_policies_En.pdf

National Audit Office. (2021, December 10). Regulation of Private Renting. Department for Levelling Up, Housing & Communities. HC 863.

Nearly Legal. (2020, July 2). *F00YO154. Redacted County Court Judgement. County Court at York*. [online]. Available from: http://nearlylegal.co.uk/wp-content/uploads/2020/07/20.07.02-Redacted-Court-Order.pdf?utm_source=mailpoet&utm_medium=email&utm_campaign=new-on-nearly-legal-newsletter-total-new-posts_1

Norfolk Constabulary. (2019). Freedom of Information Request Reference No: FOI 004622/18. (January 2019). www.norfolk.police.co.uk; [online]. Available from: https://www.norfolk.police.uk/sites/norfolk/files/4622_-_jan_-_offences_under_eviction_act.pdf

Peaker G. (2020). *Discrimination and 'No DSS.' Nearly Legal*. (14 July 2020). [online]. Available from: https://nearlylegal.co.uk/2020/07/discrimination-and-no-dss/

Police Community. (2012). Police Visual Handbook. General Policing Forum. (13 January 2012). [online]. Available from: https://police.community/topic/237132-police-visual-handbook/

Ratcliffe, P. (2002). 'Theorising Ethnic and 'Racial' Exclusion in Housing. Race', in *Housing and Social Exclusion*. London: Jessica Kingsley, pp. 22–39.

Reeve, K., Cole, I., Batty, E., Foden, M., Green, S. and Pattison, B. (2016, July). 'Home No Less Will Do. Sheffield Hallam University. Centre for Regional Economic and Social Research', *Crisis*.

Reeve-Lewis, B., Bolton, J.L. and Rugg, J. (2022, May). *Offences Under the Protection from Eviction Act 1977 in England and Wales: A Report from Safer Renting*. London: Safer Renting. Cambridge House.

Richards, G. and Davies, N. (2023, October 30). *Performance Tracker 2023: Criminal Courts*. Institute for Government. Available from: https://www.instituteforgovernment.org.uk/publication/performance-tracker-2023/criminal-courts

Sagoe, C., Ehrlich, R., Reynolds, L. and Rich, H. (2020). *Time for Change: Marking Renting Fairer for Private Landlords*. England, London: Shelter.

Shelter. (2020, July 14). *No DSS: Landmark Court Ruling Confirms Housing Benefit Discrimination is Unlawful*. England, London: Shelter.

Shelter. (2023, March 21). *Landmark Case Finds 'No Children' Policies Breach Letting Agent Code of Practice*. England, London: Shelter.

Spencer, R., Reeve-Lewis, B., Rugg, J. and Barata, E. (2020). *Journeys in the Shadow Private Rented Sector*. University of York: Cambridge House/Centre for Housing Policy, p. 47.

UK Parliament. (2023). *The Future of Legal Aid. House of Commons*. [online]. Available from: https://committees.parliament.uk/work/531/the-future-of-legal-aid/

Warren, J. (2023). *Met Police updates evictions guidance for officers*. BBC News, London. [online]. Available from: https://www.bbc.co.uk/news/uk-england-london-66610004

Wilson, W. (2023, October 30). *Can Private Landlords Refuse to Let to Benefit Claimants and People with Children?* London: House of Commons Library.

Work and Pensions Committee. (2019, April 24). *Oral Evidence: No DSS: Discrimination Against Benefit Claimants in the Housing Sector: HC 1995*. London: House of Commons.

World Justice Project. (2022). *Rules of Law Index; Civil Justice; United Kingdom*. [online]. Available from: https://worldjusticeproject.org/rule-of-law-index/factors/2022/United%20Kingdom/Civil%20Justice/

Work and Pensions Committee. (2014, April 2). Support for housing costs in the reformed welfare system. HC720. House of Commons. London. Available from: https://publications.parliament.uk/pa/cm201314/cmselect/cmworpen/720/720.pdf

6   Housing Policy, Cost and Implementation

This chapter considers housing policy costs and implementation in terms of expenses and gains made by the government and enforcing authorities but also the costs and gains for landlords and tenants and in as much as possible how costs are distributed over time, taking account of not just visible expenses but also those that may be hidden or gains that are non-monetised. According to Morestin (2012), both aspects, visible or hidden costs, are highly influential upon how other actors or stakeholders react to policy.

Between 2007 and 2018, the private rental population aged between 25 and 34 increased by 44%. During the same period, owner occupancy decreased by 17% amongst the same age group meaning people aged 25–34 are more likely to be private tenants than owner occupiers (MHCLG, 2019a). Between 2011 and 2017, household numbers in temporary accommodation increased by 60%. A total of £845 million was spent in 2017 on temporary accommodation with approximately £638 million funded by housing benefits (NAO, 2017). The demand for temporary accommodation for private renting households increased from 10% to 39%, between 2009 and 2017 (DLUHC, 2023a; NAO, 2017).

Local housing allowance rates are variable across council districts and based on available rental stock within specified areas. The maximum available to claim is directly related to property size, household characteristics and bedroom entitlement (Hobson, 2023; Wilson, 2023). The Department for Work and Pensions calculate Local Housing Allowance rates for private tenants across 151 broad rental market areas. The 30th percentile used to set the allowance rates with a maximum cap is based upon a survey of rents taken for 2019–2020 to enable tenants to afford the cheapest 30% of available local properties (Emmerson et al., 2020; Hobson, 2023; Wilson, 2023).

DOI: 10.1201/9781032705071-6

The VOA (2022) collected rental information on private market rents within these broad rental market areas. Table 6.1 shows the housing benefit bands classed from Categories A to E. Category A is a dwelling where the tenant has exclusive use of only one bedroom with shared use of other facilities. Category B is a dwelling where the tenant has exclusive use of only one bedroom with exclusive use of other facilities. Category C is a dwelling where the tenant has the use of only two bedrooms. Category D is a dwelling where the tenant has the use of only three bedrooms. Category E is a dwelling where the tenant has the use of only four bedrooms. The average difference in local housing allowance and the average 30th percentile rent across broad rental market areas increases from 4.3% to 5% of total monthly rent according to the band.

Local housing allowance was introduced originally to ensure equitability across local authority areas, where households in similar situations but subject to differing rents based on market forces would receive relative levels of help. An incentive was originally provided to encourage tenants to agree to rent accommodation cheaper than Local Housing Allowance rates and retain up to £15 per week to increase their income. This was removed in April 2011 (Carey and Bell, 2022; Hobson, 2023).

As seen in the chapter on equtiability, the way benefit is paid discourages landlords from letting to tenants on benefits, not helped by the government's decision to freeze Local Housing Allowance rates between 2016 and 2020 because average earnings increased by 11% over the past seven years whilst benefits increased by a greater

Table 6.1 England: Weekly Local Housing Allowance (LHA) and Average 30th Percentile Rent Across 151 Broad Rental Market Areas

Band	LHA	CI 95%	Average 30th percentile rent	CI 95%	Monthly difference	Monthly difference %
A	£79.97	[79.4, 79.9]	£83.56	[83.3, 83.8]	£15.60	4.3
B	£129.58	[128.9, 130.2]	£135.60	[134.9, 136.3]	£26.09	4.4
C	£160.53	[159.7, 161.3]	£167.48	[166.6, 168.3]	£30.12	4.6
D	£193.36	[192.3, 194.4]	£202.94	[201.8, 204.1]	£41.51	4.7
E	£252.09	[250.8, 253.4]	£265.35	[263.8, 266.9]	£57.46	5.0

Source: (Valuation Office Agency (VOA), 2022).

proportion. Jobseekers' allowance rose by 21% making it financially more advantageous in the government's view to choose not to work over employment. Freezing tax credits, local housing allowance and reducing social housing rents by 1% was intended to correct this and estimated to yield savings of £4 billion annually over the period (HM Treasury, 2015; Wilson, 2023). The freeze simply reinforced concerns about the gap between allowance subsidy and private rented sector market rents. A greater proportion of tenants in arrears are in receipt of benefits for housing support compared to those not claiming benefits (DLUHC, 2023b; Wilson, 2023). Amid concerns voiced from the Residential Landlords Association, the CLGSC (2016) called for local housing allowance levels to be reviewed and raised if necessary closer to local levels of market rents. The Residential Landlords Association complained that it was naïve of the government to simply expect landlords to ignore rising interest rates and inflation and freeze rents for four years to match the Local Housing Allowance freeze.

During the COVID-19 pandemic, local housing allowance was set at a flat rate for differing sizes of local properties across a broad market area based on the 30th percentile of market rents (VOA, 2020). In areas of high housing demand Local Housing Allowance rates fell significantly below this level widening the gap between allowance subsidy and tenant's inability to top up rental coverage, argued by landlords to be pricing benefit claimants out of the market. Subsequent increases were not in line with inflation (Wilson, 2023), another freeze was imposed between 2021 and 2026 and forecast to see the £1 billion cost of the measure in 2020–2021 shrink to £0.3 billion (Office for Budget Responsibility (OBR), 2020).

Overtime local housing allowance rates are anticipated to reduce below the 30th percentile of local rents across the board (Wilson, 2023) representing an almost £1 billion investment in Local Housing Allowance rates for 1.5 million housing benefit or housing elements of Universal Credit recipients providing them with £600 more housing support for 2020–2021 (Levelling Up, Housing and Communities Committee, 2023). Landlords will continue to take account of inflation and interest rates (CLGSC, 2016). In 2022, the base rate of borrowing was 0.25%, which increased to 5.25% in 2023 (Bank of England, 2021a, 2023) and is likely to have affected landlord's mortgage interests. It also presents a potential motivation for increasing rents or worse, exercising unlawful evictions to gain possession (Spencer and Rugg, 2023).

Category A local housing allowance for an HMO tenant is on average £346.53 per calendar month across broad rental market areas. SpareRoom (2022) estimate the average monthly room rent in the UK (excluding London) is £554.00 based on the quarterly rental index for the third quarter of 2022. A person on average Local Housing Allowance would have to make up a monthly shortfall of £208 (37%) difference of their rent through other means.

Emmerson et al. (2020) observed local housing allowance freezes applied over the previous decade left tenants in high-rental neighbourhoods with less support than those in low-rental equivalents. In 2016, the freeze was accompanied by a reduction of the benefit cap threshold to limit household total benefit entitlement to £23,000 in London and £20,000 outside London reducing levels of housing support where weekly benefits exceed this cap (Levelling Up, Housing and Communities Committee, 2023; Wilson, 2023). The application of a further freeze in 2020 was predicted to decrease the availability of affordable rental accommodation overtime because rents increase as housing stock dwindles. Available support based on 2019 market rent statistics was predicted to outdate and no longer be reflective of current market costs (Emmerson et al., 2020).

Market trends bear this prediction out during 2023 rents increased by 4.4% more compared to 4.2% in 2022. Rental housing demand increased whilst new landlord instructions decreased leaving supply unable to match demand. This will likely lead to further rental increases (Greenwood and Holt, 2010; ONS, 2023; Quigley and Raphael, 2004). The lack of affordable housing supply is a flaw in the neoliberal principle of the trickle-down effect of wealth distribution. Property values increase benefitting homeowners but to the disadvantage of private renters who must consider the transaction costs of paying higher rents for better accommodation or accepting lower standards of accommodation with lower rents to be able to afford other goods (Greenwood and Holt, 2010; Quigley and Raphael, 2004).

The government stated it is not the intention for local housing allowance rates to cover all rents in all areas, local authorities were provided with a £1.6 billion fund for discretionary housing payments to be 'spent in line with local priorities and non-statutory guidance on priority groups (Levelling Up, Housing and Communities Committee, 2023). Whilst supportive of the need to reduce dependency on benefits, Emmerson et al. (2020) remained critical of its inequitable and random manner of implementation because it replicates known problems seen previously with this approach.

From April 2017, benefit claimants with more than two children born after this date are ineligible for further housing benefit support, universal credit and tax credits (Levelling Up, Housing and Communities Committee, 2023; Wilson, 2023). In written evidence submitted to the Work and Pensions Select Committee 2016 inquiry on Universal Credit and its implementation, Residential Landlord's Association (2016) explained landlords view benefit changes and allowance freezes as a risk to their return on investment which reduces the income thresholds of prospective tenants, particularly households with families consequently disincentivising landlords from wanting to rent to these households.

Some landlords and letting agencies seek to maximise profits by charging the maximum price allowed by local housing allowance often for very small and often not fully self-contained accommodation (with shared kitchens). Sometimes, houses are cut up into collections of very small studios (HCCPA, 2022b). It is common for prices for small studios/rooms in HMO accommodations to be between £850 and £1,100 per person often poorly maintained. The highest proportion of tenants in rental arrears receives Universal Credit. This does not cover the full cost of private rent being around £225 PCM higher on average compared to social housing rents leaving private tenants vulnerable to arrears, with very little left on which to exist. Universal credit promotes a cycle of poverty and benefit dependency. Recipients are reluctant to return to employment fearing homelessness because of the effect working has on benefits which either cease or decrease despite tenants still having high rents to pay (Carey and Bell, 2022; HCCPA, 2022a, 2022b).

One of the main barriers preventing renters from becoming homeowners is the difficulties in raising enough money for a 5% deposit. Private renters responding to the EHS 2020–2021 on average were spending 31% of household income on rent. In comparison, social renters spend 27% whilst owner occupiers spend 18% on mortgages (DLUHC, 2021a). Home ownership between 1910 and 1990 was traditionally driven by house prices being approximately three or four times the average earnings enabling first-time buyers to save for 3–4 years and buy whilst still in their twenties. It now takes over a decade to save for a deposit, in London, it could be as high as 30 years (Burn-Murdoch, 2024; Generation Rent, 2023). The Bank of England (2021b) found this affects 83% of private tenants unable to save. A further 6% can raise a deposit but cannot meet the financial conduct authority's affordability test to become first-time buyers. In America and the UK, housing affordability influences population age structures. For homeowners, house price increases have a positive effect on fertility rates prompting moves to larger homes as families grow but declines amongst non-homeowners. For English private renters, a 10% house price increase is associated with a 4.9% fall in birth rate most notably amongst tenants aged 20–29 (Aksoy, 2016; Dettling and Kearney, 2014).

During 2021–2022, the Tenancy Deposit Scheme (TDS) protected approximately 1.8 million deposits with over 459,000 registrants to a value of over £2 billion (DLUHC, 2022b; TDS, 2022). During the same period, the TDS-free dispute resolution service resolved over 14,000 deposit disputes (TDS, 2022). The DLUHC (2022b) using EHS data from 2018–2019 estimated the proportion of private rented sector households covered by the TDS scheme is between 45% and 66%. Around 6% of tenants claim their deposits are not protected and a further 18% did not know either way.

In 2019 when surveyed about the use of TDSs, 96% of landlords and agents combined confirmed most recent deposits were registered. Of the landlords who responded 67% confirmed using the scheme whilst 17% said they did not use them; 57.5% of landlords and agents surveyed either retained the deposit or partly refunded due to property damage. Sixty-five per cent said it was also to cover cleaning costs before re-letting. Other reasons given were tenants' failure to maintain the property or to cover unpaid rent or for disposal costs of items left behind (MHCLG, 2019b). Many landlords do not take deposits, the scheme became mandatory in 2007 and many long-standing tenancies commencing before that time are not covered. The DLUHC claim it is currently impossible to determine exactly how many landlords are potentially flouting the law. Forty five percent of landlords raise rent for new tenancies. Thirty-five per cent kept rent at the same rate whilst 8% said they decreased it. The remaining 12% let for the first time. For tenancy renewals, 64% of landlords maintained the same rent whilst 26% increased it. Four per cent decreased rent on renewal (DLUHC, 2022b).

A total of 889,000 (20%) of private renting occupiers subsidise rent payments with housing benefits, including people who work but receive some housing benefit (MHCLG, 2019a). Between 2020 and 2021, approximately 335,000 private renting households were in rental arrears. Over 33% owed between one and two months' rent (DLUHC, 2021b;

MHCLG, 2021). In April 2023, the benefit cap thresholds increased by 10.1% in line with inflation-linked social security benefits (Levelling Up, Housing and Communities Committee, 2023; Wilson, 2023). Despite the intention for dependency on Local Housing Allowance to decrease (Hobson, 2023) between May 2022 and May 2023, there was a 19.5% increase in the number of UK households claiming Universal Credit with housing entitlement representing 35% of the total number of Universal Credit claimants (DWP, 2023). An increase of 54% from pre-COVID levels recorded up to February 2020 (Abrey, 2021; DWP, 2023).

In 2021, around 159,000 people in lower-income groups receiving debt advice from StepChange had significant rental arrears. A total of 54,000 (35%) were private rented sector tenants, 25,000 households had children and 24% were single parents (5,200 were in rent arrears). Fifty per cent of tenants had additional vulnerabilities such as mental or physical health issues (this increased to 62% amongst those in rent arrears). A significant proportion struggled to pay bills and maintain ongoing essential expenditures. Those in rental arrears were all particularly vulnerable to no-fault evictions or eviction for two months arrears. Thirty-eight per cent of private rented sector tenants in the lowest quality of housing lacked energy efficiency measures or had poor conditions exacerbating cold reportedly spent more income on energy bills (HCCPA, 2022a).

The Office of National Statistics (ONS, 2023) monitor price data annually from a proportion of private rented sector properties tracking differences in rental costs over time. Compared to February 2022 where rent increased by 36%, recent data shows an increase of 50.6% with increases being notably higher in London and lowest in the North West. The average rental increase across the country in 2023 was 9.7% and lowest in the Midlands at 8.2%. London-based tenants experienced higher rental increases at 12%. In London, 33.3% of rented properties revisited showed rental increases of over 10%, almost double the proportion found across England where the same effect was found in 18.2% of stock sampled. The highest rental increases in London were found amongst flats and maisonettes. The price increases are likely to have occurred during contract renewal at the ending of a fixed period, or upon change of tenancy.

Landlords surveyed in 2018 (MHCLG, 2019b) mostly funded their acquisitions through buy-to-let mortgages with average gross rental incomes of £15,000 (before tax) mostly making up 42% of total annual gross income. Up to 61% of landlords earned a gross income of up to £20,000 per annum. The remaining 41% earned an annual gross rental income anywhere between £20,000 and above £50,000. From September 2022, the government increased the stamp duty surcharge for second homes by 3% on top of existing thresholds. Ordinarily, a person buying a single property pays no tax on values up to £250,000. A landlord buying a second home pays 3% (£7,500). For properties worth up to £925,000, the proportion between £250,000 and £925,000 for a single property ordinary rate would be 5%, but for landlords buying a second property, this is 8%. Properties worth up to £1.5 million incur the first two tax rates and a further cost of 13% to a landlord, whereas the ordinary rate would be 10%. For properties above £1.5 million, the ordinary applicable rate is 12%, but for a landlord, this increases to 15% (GOV.UK, n.d.).

Costs to landlords creating a new tenancy agreement are on average £500 including reference checks, cleaning and inventory fees (agency fees and marketing are extra). Periodic tenancies under the now defunct Renters (Reform) Bill presented the possibility of tenants giving two months' notice upon the date of the tenancy commencement. To LARG (2023), short-term lets are not cost-effective. Longer terms allow set-up costs to be defrayed, whereas a trend in shorter terms would lead to substantially higher increases in market rent along with increased financial costs for mortgages of over £250 per month, higher utility bills and maintenance expenses all of which are causing landlords with small portfolios to exit the market because it's no longer profitable (Propertymark, 2023).

From April 2017, the government imposed a phased-in restriction on tax relief for landlords. Previously, landlords were able to deduct mortgage interest under allowable expenses after rental profit. This was gradually reduced between 2017 and 2020: in 25%, deductions from 75% allowable to zero. Tax relief is applicable up to the first £11,850 of earnings, then rental profit and any salary from other employment is taxed at 20%. However, there remains an allowable expense claim of up to £7,000 (HM Revenue & Customs, 2016).

A study of the London housing market observed costs to the UK healthcare system arising from poor housing and health-related outcomes such as 'disrepair and mental health and wellbeing' are almost as much as the health care cost burden arising from smoking and alcohol-related disease (Petersen et al., 2022), which is estimated to be £2.5 billion per annum (O'Connor, 2017). The Building Research

Establishment found annual treatment costs for patients exposed to poor housing conditions is £1.4 billion per annum (Garrett et al., 2021).

Garrett et al. (2021) point out that the initial £1.4 billion cost only accounts for the first year of treatment and not ongoing medical costs beyond this point. When societal costs are considered, described as ongoing care and loss of economic potential through less productivity, poorer educational attainment and reduced career prospects, the annual cost is estimated to be £18.5 billion. In a poll commissioned by Shelter (2021), private renting tenants reported health impacts concerning fear of eviction have a negative effect on their work. Twenty-one per cent continuously struggle to pay rent, a further 26% are often unable to heat their homes. Most commonly societal costs arise through exposure to the hazard of excess cold as well as accidents such as falls on stairs. There are associated mental health costs arising from suffering and trauma (Garrett et al., 2021).

The NAO estimate approximately £9.3 billion in rent is paid annually to private landlords whose rental properties fail the decent homes standard, for which the government currently funds landlords through housing benefits to an annual amount of £3 billion in welfare subsidy (DLUHC, 2022a). The government believed reformations under the now defunct Renters (Reform) Bill would prevent landlords from benefitting from this income stream through renting non-decent homes to vulnerable benefit-dependent occupiers (DLUHC, 2022b, 2023c). Citizens Advice (2023) reported clients complaining about exposure to damp and mould in their homes waited over a year for landlords to adequately resolve the issues. Through the Renters (Reform) Bill, the government hoped remedial improvements would lead to NHS savings of up to £340 million annually on treating health issues related to poor property conditions in welfare-subsidised housing (DLUHC, 2022b, 2023c; Marmot, 2020; NAO, 2021).

EHS data from 2017–2018 show the average length of residency in a private rented sector dwelling is 4.1 years. Forty-five per cent of tenants privately rented for less than five years, 25% had been renting between five and nine years and 26% for more than ten years. In the 12 months before the survey, the largest number of persons moving house occurred within the private rented sector; 860,000 households moved between rental accommodation. A total of 219,000 new rental households were created and 98,000 moved from owner occupancy to rental accommodation, some 208,000 households moved out of renting into owner occupancy (MHCLG, 2019a).

Previously, 18% of tenants felt that proposed three-year tenancies would make rental increases more affordable because the longer stability provided would offset frequent costs of moving and payment of deposits (MHCLG, 2018). Families in the private rented sector are estimated to incur approximately £1,514 in moving costs each time they relocate (Shelter, 2023). Tenants facing the expense of moving also take on additional debt when renting new properties. Forty-five per cent of landlords surveyed in 2021 indicated they increase rent for new tenants (DLUHC, 2022b, 2023c). In the same survey, 64% of landlords said they did not increase rent when renewing tenancies for existing tenants. The government believed that if Section 21 evictions were abolished it would reduce the frequency of moves producing savings for renters and easing financial pressures owing to the stronger security of tenure brought about through the ban. Further savings could come from not having to pay higher rents when moving (DLUHC, 2022b).

Higher rents add to financial pressures facing tenants when relocating making it more difficult for prospective first-time buyers to save for deposits or spend on heating and food. The government is concerned tenants in this situation may 'trade down' accepting smaller-sized accommodation unsuitable for their needs to pay lower rents. Such conditions could lead to negative health impacts, employment issues and loss of productivity (DLUHC, 2023c).

The MHCLG found the median time for landlords to gain possession through the courts is 16.3 weeks. This was disputed by landlords who claim it is between 21 and 52 weeks. The cost to landlords in terms of legal fees and loss of rental income is between £1,000 and £5,000. Over 50% of cases resulting in possession orders being granted took seven weeks. Around three out of four possession claims do not reach the final stage because occupiers often leave voluntarily (MHCLG, 2018, 2019b).

Costs for landlords to appeal at the tribunal to challenge local authority enforcement actions are considerably lower, but a local authority preparing a defence against an appeal over a civil financial penalty incurs considerably higher costs, estimated on average to be £5,000 per case taking 16 working days of officer time to complete at the opportunity cost of other work (CIEH, 2023; HCCPA, 2022c).

In 2019, ongoing reformations to court procedures were forecast to deliver £2.3 billion in efficiency savings by reducing operating costs and digitising paper-based procedures, but the project's end has been increasingly delayed, owing to the underestimation of the scale and complexity of the project, and consequently, savings are now anticipated to be £310 million lower than forecast (HCCPA, 2023).

According to Bolt Burdon Kemp LLP (2023) and Makinson (2021), the Legal Aid, Sentencing and Punishment of Offenders Act (2012) saw the £2 billion legal aid budget reduce by £350 million. Between 2011 and 2020, England's average annual legal aid expenditure was highest within the poorest areas of London, £242,051 p.a. 95% CI (242,025; 242,078), North West £96,191 p.a. 95% CI (96,156; 96,228) and Yorkshire and the Humber £94,684 p.a. 95% CI (94,682; 94,688). Expenditure is attributed to the prevalence of available regional legal aid service providers and high service demand for cases within the eligible scope of legal aid provisions such as eviction and environmental law.

A parliamentary inquiry (UK Parliament, 2023) heard oral evidence concerning the effect of poor pay for criminal defence lawyers not being commensurate to the hours spent on case work because fee rates have not increased in over 14 years. In real terms, criminal defence lawyers with around 15 years' experience earn less than when they started. This has seen a deskilling in some areas of law with Barristers leaving the profession. An independent review carried out by Bellamy (2021) argued fees must increase by 15% (£135 million p.a.) at minimum, whereas the government proposed an 11% increase (UK Parliament, 2023). Strike action by Barristers ensued exacerbating delays in court proceedings. The strike ended in October 2022 with concessions for a 15% rate rise across most criminal cases (Richards and Davies, 2023).

Despite this, Barristers feel capacity is limited or overstretched and has worsened over the past year. Changes made to legal aid that took work away from criminal defence lawyers saw many barristers diversify legal work away from criminal cases. Retention remains an issue (Bellamy, 2021; Richards and Davies, 2023; UK Parliament, 2023). Spending on criminal cases since 2011–2012 declined by 43% and full-time criminal barristers declined by 9.8% between 2017 and 2022 (Richards and Davies, 2023).

The government hoped that the now defunct Renters (Reform) Bill would provide longer security of tenure and declining levels of household moves. This would adversely impact upon the business models of managing agents and was estimated to cost each letting agent approximately £1,200 per annum (DLUHC, 2023c). Private renters were the group thought most likely to financially benefit from the bill's provisions;

having not incurred frequent moving costs or repercussions from displacement. Tenant households would have benefitted by at least £21 per year. Landlords would also benefit from a £7 saving annually per rented property in agency fees owing to less churn in tenancies as well as a reduction in void periods. Tenants would also benefit from paying rent for a better-maintained property or more efficient mechanisms for dispute resolution where necessary (DLUHC, 2023c).

In the current market where choice of housing is scarce, landlords can set market prices regularly evict and raise rents, taking advantage of a shrinking market. Agents benefit from constant churn and letting costs. For landlords, the base rate of borrowing and interest rates impact mortgages, but these costs are easily absorbed into rental increases. In areas of high demand, landlords benefit through policy capture and local authority reliance on their housing provision to discharge homeless duty, guaranteeing income for landlords through benefits who can charge the maximum rate whilst circumventing repairs and maintenance costs.

If a local authority attempts enforcement of repairs, the cost of a tribunal appeal is disproportionately negligible for Landlords compared to costs incurred by local authorities in defending their decisions. Facing increasing benefits and temporary accommodation costs the government responded by freezing allowance rates or keeping them below inflation levels. Tenants paying high rents risk eviction for arrears or no-fault evictions. This increases the very homeless and temporary accommodation demand costs the freeze was intended to save on. The stress of eviction under these circumstances or worse, illegal eviction is increasing health care costs related to poor housing which is poorly addressed by local authorities due to cuts and lack of resources.

Although the Renters (Reform) Bill is no more it shows us that a reformatory policy aimed at reducing displacement and increasing security of tenure, can only work if tenants are able to afford rent and are able to live in properties that do not place their health at risk, long-term rental capacity could be freed up by enabling more renters to afford to buy.

References

Abrey, R. (2021, August 17). *Warning Issued Over Impact of Benefit Cuts on Renters*. National Residential Landlords Association. [online]. Available from: https://www.nrla.org.uk/news/warning-issued-over-impact-of-benefit-cuts-on-renters

Aksoy, C.G. (2016, September). Short-Term Effects of House Prices on Birth Rates. EBRD, Working Paper No. 192. Available from: http://dx.doi.org/10.2139/ssrn.2846173

Bank of England. (2021a). Bank Rate increased to 0.25% – December 2021. Monetary Policy Committee Meeting.

Bank of England. (2021b). 'Financial Stability Report', *Financial Policy Committee,* December.

Bank of England. (2023). Bank Rate Maintained at 5.25% – September 2023. Monetary Policy Committee Meeting.

Bellamy, C. (2021, November 29). 'Independent Review of Criminal Legal Aid', *GOV.UK.* [online]. Available from: https://www.gov.uk/government/groups/independent-review-of-criminal-legal-aid#:~:text=The%20Independent%20Review%20of%20Criminal,the%20Lord%20Chancellor%20in%202021.

Bolt Burdon Kemp LLP. (2023). *Inequality within Britain's Legal Aid Funding System.* [online]. Available from: https://www.bolt-burdonkemp.co.uk/our-insights/campaigns/inequality-in-britains-legal-aid-funding-system/

Burn-Murdoch, J. (2024). 'The Housing Crisis is Still Being Under-played', *Financial Times*, 13 January. Available from: https://www.ft.com/content/f21642d8-da2d-4e75-886e-2b7c1645f063

Carey, M. and Bell, S. (2022). 'Universal Credit, Lone Mothers and Poverty: Some Ethical Challenges for Social Work with Children and Families', *Ethics and Social Welfare*, 16(1), pp. 3–18.

Chartered Institute of Environmental Health (CIEH). (2023, November). Written Evidence. House of Commons Public Bill Committee. Renters (Reform) Bill. RRB50.

Citizens Advice. (2023, February 9). 'Damp, Cold and Full of Mould', *The Reality of Housing in the Private Rented Sector*. [online]. Available from: https://www.citizensadvice.org

Communities and Local Government Select Committee. (2016, August 18). *Homelessness. Third Report of Session 2016–17: HC 40.* London: House of Commons.

Department for Levelling Up, Housing and Communities. (2021a, December 9). *English Housing Survey 2020 to 2021: Headline Report.* London.

Department for Levelling Up, Housing and Communities. (2021b, October 13). *Household Resilience Study: Wave 3 April-May 2021.* London: English Housing Survey.

Department for Levelling Up, Housing and Communities. (2022a, June 16). *A Fairer Private Rented Sector*. London: DLUHC.

Department for Levelling Up, Housing and Communities. (2022b, May 26). *English Private Landlord Survey 2021*. London: DLUHC.

Department for Levelling Up, Housing and Communities. (2023a, October 13). *Statutory Homelessness in England: Financial Year 2022–23*. London: DLUHC.

Department for Levelling Up, Housing and Communities. (2023b, July 13). *English Housing Survey 2021 to 2022: Private Rented Sector*. London: DLUHC.

Department for Levelling Up, Housing and Communities. (2023c, May 12). *Renters (Reform) Bill Impact Assessment: DLUHC 2564*. London: DLUHC.

Department for Work and Pensions. (2023). 'UC Households 3 – Month by Housing Entitlement', *Stat-xplore. dwp.gov.uk*. [online]. Available from: https://stat-xplore.dwp.gov.uk/webapi/jsf/tableView/tableView.xhtml#

Dettling, L.J. and Kearney, M.S. (2014) 'House Prices and Birth Rates: The Impact of the Real Estate Market on the Decision to Have a Baby', *Journal of Public Economics*, 110, pp. 82–100.

Emmerson, C., Johnson, P., Stockton, I., Waters, T. and Zaranko, B. (2020, November 25). *Initial Reaction from IFS Researchers on Spending Review 2020 and OBR Forecasts*. Institute for Fiscal Studies. [online]. Available from: https://ifs.org.uk/news/initial-reaction-ifs-researchers-spending-review-2020-and-obr-forecasts

Garrett, H., Mackay, M. and Nicol, S. (2021). *The Cost of Poor Housing in England*. Watford, UK: BRE Group.

Generation Rent. (2023, July 3). *Saving for a Mortgage Deposit Now Takes a Decade*. Available from: https://www.generationrent.org/2023/07/03/saving-for-a-mortgage-deposit-now-takes-a-decade/

Greenwood, D.T. and Holt, R.P.F. (2010) 'Growth, Inequality and Negative Trickle Down', *Journal of Economic Issues*, 44(2), pp. 403–410.

Gov.UK (n.d.) Stamp Duty Land Tax. Available from: https://www.gov.uk/stamp-duty-land-tax/residential-property-rates

HM Revenue & Customs. (2016, July, 20). *Tax relief for residential landlords: how it's worked out*. (Last updated 6 April 2017). GOV.UK Available at; https://www.gov.uk/guidance/changes-to-tax-relief-for-residential-landlords-how-its-worked-out-including-case-studies

HM Treasury. (2015, July 8). *Summer Budget 2015: HC 264*. London: House of Commons.

Hobson, F. (2023, March 9). *Local Housing Allowance (LHA): Help with Rent for Private Tenants*. House of Commons. [online]. Available from: https://researchbriefings.files.parliament.uk/documents/SN04957/SN04957.pdf

House of Commons Committee of Public Accounts. (2022a, January). Written Evidence Submitted by StepChange Debt Charity. PRP0005.

House of Commons Committee of Public Accounts. (2022b, January). Written Evidence Submitted by Glass Door Homeless Charity. PRP0006.

House of Commons Committee of Public Accounts. (2022c, January). Written Evidence Submitted by Association of Chief Environmental Health Officers in England. PRP0002.

House of Commons Committee of Public Accounts. (2023, June 30). *Progress on the Courts and Tribunals Reform Programme: HC 1002*. London: House of Commons.

Large Agents Representation Group (LARG). (2023, November). Written Evidence. House of Commons Public Bill Committee. Renters (Reform) Bill. RRB17

Legal Aid, Sentencing and Punishment of Offenders Act 2012 c.10. Available from: https://www.legislation.gov.uk/ukpga/2012/10/contents/enacted (accessed 22 October 2023).

Levelling Up, Housing and Communities Committee. (2023, October 20). *Reforming the Private Rented Sector: Government's Response to the Committee's Fifth Report of Session 2022–23: HC 1935*. London: House of Commons.

Makinson, R. (2021, August 26). 'LASPO: How A Near-Decade of Legal Aid Cuts Has Affected Britain's Most Vulnerable', *Lawyer Monthly*. [online]. Available from: https://www.lawyer-monthly.com/2021/08/laspo-how-a-near-decade-of-legal-aid-cuts-has-affected-britains-most-vulnerable/

Marmot, M. (2020, February 25). 'Health Equity in England: The Marmot Review 10 Years on', *BMJ*, 368.

Ministry of Housing Communities and Local Government (2018a) *Overcoming the barriers to longer tenancies in the private rented sector*. (Updated 15 April 2019). [online]. Available from: https://www.gov.uk/government/consultations/overcoming-the-barriers-to-longer-tenancies-in-the-private-rented-sector

Ministry of Housing Communities and Local Government. (2019a). *English Housing Survey Headline Report 2017–18*. London: MHCLG.

Ministry of Housing Communities and Local Government. (2019b, January). *English Private Landlord Survey 2018*. London: MHCLG.

Ministry of Housing Communities and Local Government. (2021, April 21). *Household Resilience Study: Wave 2 November-December 2020*. London: English Housing Survey.

Morestin, F. (2012, September). *A Framework for Analyzing Public Policies: Practical Guide*. National Collaborating Centre for Healthy Public Policy. [online]. Available from: http://www.ncchpp.ca/docs/Guide_framework_analyzing_policies_En.pdf

National Audit Office. (2017). 'Report – Value for money, Homelessness', *www.nao.org.uk*. [online]. Available from: https://www.nao.org.uk/reports/homelessness/

National Audit Office. (2021, December 10). *Regulation of Private Renting: HC 863*. London: Department for Levelling Up, Housing & Communities.

O'Connor, R. (2017, October 4). *Health Matters: Preventing Ill Health from Alcohol and Tobacco Use*. Health Matters, UK Health Security Agency. [online]. Available from: https://ukhsa.blog.gov. uk/2017/10/04/health-matters-preventing-ill-health-from-alcohol-and-tobacco-use/

Office for Budget Responsibility. (2020, November 25). *Economic and Fiscal Outlook – November 2020*. Available from: https://obr. uk/efo/economic-and-fiscal-outlook-november-2020/

Office for National Statistics. (2023, January 15). *Index of Private Housing Rental Prices, UK: January 2023*. London: Office for National Statistics.

Petersen, J., Alexiou, A., Brewerton, D., Cornelsen, L., Courtin, E., Cummins, S., Marks, D., Seguin, M., Stewart, J., Thompson, K. and Egan, M. (2022) 'Impact of Selective Licensing Schemes for Private Rental Housing on Mental Health and Social Outcomes in Greater London, England: A Natural Experiment Study', *BMJ Open*, 12(12), p. e065747.

Propertymark. (2023, November). Written Evidence. House of Commons Public Bill Committee. Renters (Reform) Bill. RRB48.

Quigley, J.M. and Raphael, S. (2004) 'Is Housing Unaffordable? Why Isn't It More Affordable?', *The Journal of Economic Perspectives*, 18(1), pp. 191–214.

Residential Landlord's Association. (2016, February 22). Written Evidence Submitted by the Residential Landlord's Association [HOL 111].

Richards, G. and Davies, N. (2023, October 30). *Performance Tracker 2023: Criminal Courts*. Institute for Government. Available from: https://www.instituteforgovernment.org.uk/publication/performance-tracker-2023/criminal-courts

Shelter. (2021, October 13). *Health of One in Five Renters Harmed by Their Home*. England: Shelter. [online]. Available from: https://england.shelter.org.uk/media/press_release/health_of_ one_in_five_renters_harmed_by_their_home

Shelter. (2023, November). Written Evidence. House of Commons Public Bill Committee. Renters (Reform) Bill. RRB09.

SpareRoom. (2022). 'Average Rent in the UK', *spareoom.co.uk*. [online]. Available from: https://www.spareroom.co.uk/content/info-landlords/average-rent-uk/

Spencer, R. and Rugg, J. (2023, November). *Offences Under the Protection from Eviction Act 1977 in England- 2022 Update of the Annual Count, Safer Renting*. Available from: https://ch1889.org/wp-content/uploads/2023/12/PfEA-2022-offences-count-Safer-Renting-11-2023.pdf

Tenancy Deposit Scheme. (2022). 'Dispute Service. Annual Review 2021–2022', *www.thedisputeservice.co.uk.* [online]. Available from: https://www.tenancydepositscheme.com/wp-content/uploads/2022/10/Annual-Review-2021-22.pdf

UK Parliament. (2023). *The Future of Legal Aid.* House of Commons. [online]. Available from: https://committees.parliament.uk/work/531/the-future-of-legal-aid/

Valuation Office Agency (2020, January 30). *Local Housing Allowance (LHA) rates applicable from April 2020 to March 2021 – amendment as instructed by The Social Security (Coronavirus) (Further Measures) Regulations 2020.* Valuation Office Agency. London.

Valuation Office Agency. (2022, January 31). *Local Housing Allowance (LHA) Rates.* London: Valuation Office Agency.

Wilson, W. (2023, October 30). *Can Private Landlords Refuse to Let to Benefit Claimants and People with Children?* London: House of Commons Library.

7 Housing Policy Implementation, Feasibility and Acceptability

In this chapter, feasibility and acceptability are combined to evaluate the practicalities and acceptability of policy implementation and gauge the extent to which policy is judged to be tolerated by relevant stakeholders and how well resources could accommodate and administrate policy through existing mechanisms. The level of collaboration between different actors has a pivotal impact upon feasibility. The more numerous these aspects are the more complex reconciliation is with stated aims and objectives. This is dependent upon relationships between externalities and the understanding of different actors as to how their beliefs, comprehension, ethics and own objectives influence their degree of acceptance (Morestin, 2012). Homelessness and insecurity of tenure are social issues that current legislative interventions are not sufficiently addressing (ACORN, 2023; Crisis, 2023; DLUHC, 2023a; Spencer et al., 2020). There are a few actors involved in the policy's implementation including local authorities, housing lawyers, tenant support groups and the yet-to-be-established property Ombudsman. The actors affected by the policy under consideration are tenants, landlords and managing agents.

During the passage of the now defunct Renters (Reform) Bill, abolition of section 21 was suspended pending court reformation, clearly illustrating the required human and technological resources for this policy to be feasible are unavailable. Court reformation was never part of the bill, but landlords felt this unresolved externality made the bill unworkable. Rather than attempting to reform existing structures, the Centre for Social Justice believes establishing a new sufficiently resourced housing court would be more efficient. The effectiveness of any future reformations should be monitored and, if necessary, the idea of creating a separate court be revisited if progress is not made (APPG-PRS, 2023).

DOI: 10.1201/9781032705071-7

Efficient court systems were essential because proposed amendments to Section 13 of the Housing Act 1988 would have allowed tenants to appeal rental increases before a tribunal, potentially inviting numerous future cases needing to be heard (Smith, 2023). The Law Society (2022) reported in October 2022, there were 63,121 cases in backlog. They surveyed 500 solicitors working in courts and tribunals who felt cases could have been heard with more staff investment and the reopening of closed courts.

Court procedures are not instantaneous, in the past year, 47% of solicitors surveyed reported cases were delayed or adjourned. Theoretically, following the required two-month notification periods under the Renters (Reform) Bill for rental increases, any pending tribunal appeals could potentially have been delayed for four to six months. A larger influx of cases brought about by the Bill could further increase delays (The Law Society, 2022; Smith, 2023). Quilter-Pinner and Khan (2023) believe delays are underestimated because data does not capture the complexities peculiar to any given case and believe it could take up to a decade for waiting times to reduce to pre-pandemic levels.

The lengthy appeal process for challenging rental increases as proposed under the now defunct Renters (Reform) Bill would mean the amounts disputed would have fallen behind the market when finally resolved. Whilst many landlords choose not to increase rent during a tenancy, such delays may cause them to reconsider implementing rental increases within tenancies as a standard business practice to offset potential eight-month delays. Additionally, the imposition of in-tenancy rental increases could simply be used to force tenants to move out, effectively becoming a no-fault eviction by stealth (Citizens Advice, 2023; Smith, 2023).

American legal studies show an imbalance within U.S. court processes because tenants are less likely than landlords to be legally represented. Tenants lose in over 95% of eviction cases (Gold, 2016; Lonegrass, 2015; Steinberg, 2015, Tsai et al., 2020). When landlords appear unrepresented, they benefit disproportionately from legal advice, in comparison to unrepresented tenants. For tenants, success relies upon showing the landlords' actions are retaliatory. Legally represented tenants have more successful outcomes because defence lawyers know how to use this in rebuttal whereas untrained tenants do not. Lawyers familiar with procedural rules and court decorum argue points of law and negotiate settlements better than untrained tenants (Lonegrass, 2015; Steinberg, 2015).

In the UK, the imbalance is mirrored through the policy decisions to cut legal aid expenditure over the past decade and the decline in criminal defence lawyers whose income has decreased in real terms (Bolt Burdon Kemp LLP, 2023; Makinson, 2021; UK Parliament, 2023). Many landlords prefer Section 21 no-fault evictions for convenience even if there are grounds under Section 8 for arrears. Many cases go uncontested by tenants owing to poor understanding of their legal entitlements, inability to access legal advice, fear of court or fear of legal costs (Burns and Hadfield, 2018). Landlords evicting tenants in arrears or who break their agreement prefer Section 21 because, unlike other available grounds for possession, it does not require evidence, other grounds are considered insufficiently adaptable to accommodate changing situations (MHCLG, 2018).

Lacking sufficient staff to process court cases on sitting days significantly contributes to court delays. Between 2010 and 2022, Magistrate's numbers declined by 53.6%, owing to recruitment freezes despite a 2022 recruitment drive resulting in 830 magistrates a 7% increase falling far short of its intended target of 4,000 (Richards and Davies, 2023). These factors place tenants on low incomes requiring legal advice at a disadvantage in our legal system (Bolt Burdon Kemp LLP, 2023; Makinson, 2021; UK Parliament, 2023).

Legal professionals surveyed felt this could be addressed by appointing solicitors or barristers as magistrates (The Law Society, 2022). Retention of judges and magistrates was attempted by raising their retirement ages by five years. Fee-paid judges increased by 15 whilst salary-paid judges declined by 13 overall leaving numbers of judges and magistrates below 2010–2011 levels. Recruitment of circuit judges remains an acute problem notably within London and Midland crown court circuits (Richards and Davies, 2023).

The DLUHC (2022a) found that 74% of English landlords want to simplify repossessions and court processes. The dangers of simplification in an understaffed and poorly resourced court system are best illustrated through American studies. Owing to similar staffing and financial issues American housing eviction hearings are brief often lasting no more than two minutes. In Chicago, cases last on average 1 minute and 44 seconds, but longer for tenants with legal representation. In Baltimore, over 150,000 eviction cases are filed annually taking 30 seconds on average to hear, allocated to only one judge per court day (Hartman and Robinson, 2003; Gold, 2016; Lonegrass, 2015). There is insufficient time to gather thoughts and rebut landlords' arguments.

If not prompted by the judge to provide a defence, tenants are often unaware when the appropriate moment arrives for them to speak. It is highly likely that hearings at that speed gloss over many procedural errors lacking basic due processes (Lonegrass, 2015). In many cases, the convention of case dismissal where landlords fail to attend is often not followed. Often judges don't check whether eviction notices were served correctly; a general presumption prevails without examination that the facts of the landlords' case were made out. The extent to which this affects outcomes is contested, given that most cases are evictions for rental arrears; however, for tenants, the experience often feels rushed and pointless. Judges come across to tenants as inpatient and biased towards landlords (Doran et al., 2003; Lonegrass, 2015).

One of the reasons Landlords in England want simplified court procedures is fear of incurring further costs owing to the expense, time and difficulties involved in court hearings (DLUHC, 2022a). Landlords are distrustful of the judicial process; over half surveyed in 2018 perceived it was heavily biased in tenants' favour. According to the Residential Landlord Association, 46% of members struggled to gain possession. Whilst many more members had no experience of this, they were influenced by the views of those who had, thus perpetuating a 'negative perception' of lawful eviction procedures (MHCLG, 2018). Many landlords incur delays through errors made in their own applications (Burns and Hadfield, 2018).

Generation Rent feels that strengthening the law will enable mutual trust between landlords and tenants but in its last iteration, tenant support groups believed the Renters (Reform) Bill left these mechanisms potentially open to abuse (APPG-PRS, 2023; Citizens Advice, 2023; LGA, 2023). The NAO (2021) found approximately 1.5 million private landlords in England are motivated by variable circumstances, diverse portfolio sizes, property types and types of tenants. Understanding landlord incentives and behaviours and their reactions to different approaches is important when creating regulatory strategies. Given the size of the sector and obligations that were to be imposed by the Renters (Reform) Bill (2023) upon landlords to update the property register, it was never clarified exactly how local authorities can oversee compliance with eviction carried out based upon Grounds 1 and 1(a) of the Housing Act 1988, either because the landlord or their family members want to move in and make the property their primary home, or eviction is required to sell the house. Both grounds would have prevented rental marketing for a minimum of three months, Shelter envisioned some landlords leaving properties empty and re-letting after three months without any serious intention of selling or allowing family to occupy, making the provisions ineffective and facilitating retaliatory evictions by stealth as an unintended effect (APPG-PRS, 2023). Citizens Advice (2023) called for strong protections to be in place but in practical terms, local authorities are unlikely to be aware of general market buying and selling transactions or circumstances regarding vacant possession. Furthermore, the feasibility for local authorities to monitor whether re-marketing of multiple properties in these circumstances has happened within three months is doubtful unless a former occupier monitors and reports the breach, effectively meaning they were already illegally evicted. Aside from depending on renters to report irregularities there seemed to be no clear strategy. The solution would likely be a technological one using machine learning techniques that pool data and flag when such issues need enforcement input. Intelligence sharing and machine learning are used by local authorities to target licensing enforcement approaches (Moffatt, 2022) this would be something for policymakers to consider if reformation of the private rented sector is revisited.

One potential solution raised by the LGA (2023) is to require landlords to upload eviction notices for view on the property portal to allow potential oversight and ensure the three-month non-letting period is observed. However, this could unintentionally produce a public record placing tenants at a disadvantage when seeking other accommodations. In America, searchable public documents on eviction act as a deterrent to other landlords who may not wish to rent to those named evictee's (Lonegrass, 2015). The LGA (2023) and the CIEH (2023) believe the three-month pause is an insufficient amount of time for local authorities to regulate properly and should be extended to 6 months to also deter the clause from being misused. For the same reason, ACORN (2023) and Citizens Advice Newcastle and Gatesehead (2023) would have preferred to see it extended to a year.

The provisions of the Renters (Reform) Bill (2023) lacked clarity over the roles and responsibilities between the Ombudsman and local authority enforcement arms over who takes the lead particularly the risk of duplication where tenants complain to both the Ombudsman and their local authority. Lack of clarity over roles and responsibilities and insufficient resources within local authorities were key issues in poor uptake of housing enforcement under Rent Smart Wales, the Welsh government's own national registration scheme, hampered by an incapacity amongst local authorities to prosecute or issue civil financial penalties within legal time frames (CIEH, 2023; Griffiths, 2018). Just as creating licensing schemes for landlords to provide local authorities with in-date documentation does not guarantee properties operate to acceptable standards without the requisite enforcement measures (Oatt, 2019), establishing a national database requiring documentation does not guarantee national improvements in quality; this will require auditing because documentation often contains erroneous or missing elements (CIEH, 2023).

ACORN (HCCPA, 2022a) wishes to see a uniform approach towards enforcement and proper funding for councils to resource teams to deliver this. ACORN believes this can be achieved through self-funding if proper fines and enforcement orders are issued. Acceptability of new enforcement powers amongst local authorities struggling to resource enforcement is reliant upon the government to address the skills capacity in some way (DLUHC, 2023a; LGA, 2023; Wilson and Cromarty, 2023).

Enforcement legislation used by officers across different departments is dispersed across multiple legal instruments for protection from eviction, regulation of property conditions or overseeing letting agents and building and planning control enforcement. It elicits higher levels of compliance amongst landlords who are already broadly compliant but is relatively ineffective in offering protection to tenants renting from criminal landlords (Spencer et al., 2020). Propertymark (2023) are supportive of local authorities experiencing serious financial constraints being able to reinvest proceeds from financial penalties to resource enforcement but believe this is an insufficient source of funding because enforcement measures are a last resort, and the practicalities of enforcement are undermined by lack of resources and staff. Cuts and downgrading have produced a disconnect between agencies that theoretically have shared goals with some functions such as housing and anti-social behaviour teams relocated into other departments or swallowed up with other functions in large directorates (Dhesi, 2019; Spencer et al., 2020). The fragmentation of services makes it difficult for tenants to understand where to direct their complaints and is a causal factor in the ongoing prevalence of poor housing conditions in the private rented sector (Sagoe et al., 2020; Spencer et al., 2020).

For enforcement to be effective, local government requires sufficiently trained and qualified staff. A recent workforce survey (LGA,

2022) revealed 45% of local authorities struggle to recruit qualified Environmental Health Officers and 18% struggle with retention. Twenty-eight per cent cannot recruit Housing Officers, whilst 21% cannot retain them. New enforcement duties proposed under the now defunct Renters (Reform) Bill would have exerted further pressures in local authorities that lack skills capacity. There are clauses in the bill enabling the Secretary of State to fund enforcement through local authority grants. The LGA (2023) call for DLUHC to collaborate with 'sector experts to develop skills and capacity'. The CIEH (2023) state they should be used in proportion to the size of the private rental sector in each authority supporting self-funded local authority enforcement models using registration fees and financial penalties to pay for staffing and regulatory costs.

Amendments to the Housing Act 1988 under the now defunct Renters (Reform) Bill (2023) would have introduced ground 6(a) a mandatory ground requiring compliance with local authority enforcement action. An example would be where the local authority successfully applied for a banning order preventing the landlord from renting or managing a property, the landlord can evict under Section 6(a) to comply with the order (DLUHC, 2023b). Another scenario could be where a landlord applies for possession after a local authority made a prohibition order on all or part of the property. This could also be used where overcrowding is present, and the landlord needs to reduce occupancy levels to comply with the order. It will also apply where licence holders exceed the permitted occupancy levels or in cases where the landlord has not licensed a property that should be so licensed (DLUHC, 2023b; Peaker, 2023). The intention to allow landlords to evict tenants under Section 6(a) of the Housing Act 1988 to comply with local authority enforcement action has logic but is essentially 'punishing tenants for the landlord's unlawful actions' (Peaker, 2023).

Tucker (2023) observed that Ground 6(a) was absent from proposals set out in consultation papers prior to its appearance in the bill. The ability to evict when enforced upon almost rewards landlords' criminal behaviour and sanctions retaliation and is the complete opposite of the provisions under Section 33(1) of the Deregulation Act 2015 to protect tenants from retaliatory eviction. Ground 6(a) would place an extra pressure on local authorities owing to existing provisions under Sections 37 and 39 of the Land Compensation Act 1973, where if persons are displaced following the making of an order in respect of a house, building or land and they have no suitable alternative accommodation it imposes a duty on the relevant authority to find other accommodation.

In cases of overcrowding, part 1 of the Housing Act 2004 already makes provision for prohibition orders or improvement notices to be suspended to allow landlords to decant by following lawful processes to gain possession. The time scale can be extended if necessary. In situations like this, most landlords use Section 21 for convenience (DLUHC, 2022a; ODPM, 2006). The local authority can insert a trigger clause into the suspended order to ensure the order becomes live once vacant possession is accomplished. This process is also used where buildings need extensive renovation where it would be too intrusive to otherwise carry out works with occupiers in situ and allows local authorities to coordinate activities, for example around holiday periods for properties tenanted by students who would then temporarily vacate or leave altogether at the end of an academic year (Bright, 2019; Steiner v Liverpool CC, 2019; ODPM, 2006).

Ground 6(a) in the form it was written into the bill would subvert the enforcing authorities' control over these procedures possibly having a deterring effect on enforcement by local authorities. Furthermore, Ground 6(a) could lead to an impasse between tenants and landlords over complaints of disrepair. It will no longer be unlawful to evict in retaliation for a complaint because a landlord would be able to use this clause to do it lawfully or even just threaten to use it and stop the complaint from being made (Peaker, 2023; Tucker, 2023). The local authority would be obligated to rehouse under the Land Compensation Act 1973, and the enforcing officers lose the control of the management of this process afforded to them through the flexibility of the Housing Act 2004 because the tenant's removal is no longer within the enforcing authorities control but in the hands of the landlord whose offending behaviour caused the problem in the first place.

StepChange (HCCPA, 2022b) and Makinson (2021) do not see problems experienced by private rented sector clients being addressed solely through better regulation of landlords because of the inherent power imbalances and lack of protection against eviction particularly for the financially vulnerable to enforce their own basic rights. The National Residential Landlords Association (NRLA) also feel that the provision of new regulation alone is insufficient and the main driver of all the issues in the private rented sector is the lack of available homes which is something that the bill was not designed to address (APPG-PRS, 2023).

The Renters (Reform) Bill would have introduced a Decent Homes Standard for the Private Rented Sector (DLUHC, 2023a). During the passage of the Homes (Fitness for Human Habitation) Bill, regard was given to the findings of EHS (MHCLG, 2018; Wilson and Cromarty, 2018) showing large failures across the private and social rented sectors in not meeting the decent homes standard, mainly through the presence of Category 1 hazards as defined under the Housing Act 2004, lack of thermal comfort, disrepair or inadequate provision of facilities. The EHS data of 2021–2022 estimates that of the approximately 4.6 million homes in the private rented sector, 1,058,000 are currently non-decent. Further, 644,000 (14%) of these properties are believed to contain serious Category 1 hazards (DLUHC, 2022b). For the Renters (Reform) Bill to work and enable tenants to challenge landlords effectively, tenants need sufficient access to legal aid provisions and sufficient court availability to facilitate hearings (APPG-PRS, 2023; Bolt Burdon Kemp LLP, 2023; Wilson and Cromarty, 2023).

Tenants who endure prolonged exposure to poor conditions suffer mental and physical health problems when landlords fail to respond to disrepair complaints. The government believes the abolition of Section 21 and changes to Section 8 will meet the needs of tenants and landlords improving the security of tenure (HCCPA, 2022c; MHCLG, 2018). Reeve-Lewis et al. (2022) point out that even an ordinary house move is considered one of life's most stressful events, but if forcibly removed with little warning, with belongings removed or left outside, it is even more so. Illegal eviction is often the culmination of a sustained campaign of harassment over weeks which can include threats, intimidation and withholding of services such as electricity, heating, and hot water. Eviction under these circumstances or abandonment can lead to homelessness. But eviction whether lawful or illegal is traumatic emotionally and psychologically, it is a unique stressor (Hoke and Boen, 2021; Tunstall et al., 2010; Zewde et al., 2019). Even rehousing does not address the psychological distress or allow people to feel settled again (Tsai et al., 2020).

The implementation of Universal Credit still raises concerns amongst private and social landlords over the handling of arrears (Wilson, 2023). Concerns were raised in an inquiry led by the House of Commons Work and Pensions Committee (2014) that vulnerable tenants who are unable to manage their finances are not supported sufficiently well until substantial arrears have built up. The Residential Landlord's Association (2016) highlighted some of the issues in written evidence submitted to the Work and Pensions Select Committee. Universal credit and any applicable housing element are commonly paid monthly to claimants. The Residential Landlord's Association argued the procedure does nothing to allay landlords' concerns regarding the handling of arrears and in situations where landlords are requesting that payment be made directly to them. They found it very difficult to deal with the Department of Work and Pensions. Thirty-two per cent of Residential Landlords Association members surveyed described the experience as 'not very helpful at all'. According to the Residential Landlords Association, landlord's reluctance to let to prospective tenants receive benefits is partly attributable to the poor service their members have experienced from the Department of Work and Pensions (Residential Landlord's Association, 2016; Wilson, 2023).

In an updated report to the Work and Pensions Select Committee, a year later the level of dissatisfaction with the service provided by the Department of Work and Pensions amongst the members of the Residential Landlord's Association had increased to 45%. The report also stated in the past year 38% of the Landlord membership had issues with tenants on Universal Credit falling into £1600.00 worth of arrears on average. Sixty-four per cent of landlords surveyed cited rent arrears amongst Universal Credit tenants as the main reason for seeking to regain possession of a property. They also reported that 53% of landlords managed to request alternative payment methods through the Department of Work and Pensions (Residential Landlord's Association, 2017).

Research carried out in 2018 on behalf of the Residential Landlord's Association found the number of Landlords experiencing rental arrears from tenants in receipt of Universal Credit over the past year increased significantly to 61% of the membership. On average the amount of arrears accrued by Universal Credit tenants also increased to £2,390.00 and 28% of landlord members regained possession of the property as a result (Simcock, 2018). The problem was underpinned by the broader issue of the 2016 Local Housing Allowance freeze and failure to keep in step with market rents (Simcock, 2018; Wilson, 2023).

Concerns remain that ease of eviction for arrears will undermine the efforts of local authorities and supporting agencies such as Step-Change (HCCPA, 2022b) to resolve matters through debt management and that eviction for arrears should universally be accepted only as a last resort (LGA, 2023). The reluctance to rent to tenants in receipt of benefits will not overtly be able to be used to refuse a tenancy, but there remains a high reluctance amongst landlords to accept these tenants or prospective tenants who are non-UK passport holders (NAO, 2021). This presents a high risk that with nowhere else to go these tenants and their families could end up renting from the criminal landlord element (Spencer et al., 2020).

Landlords and tenants agreed that rental increases should be inflation-linked (MHCLG, 2018). Proposals to restrict rental increases to yearly under the Renters (Reform) Bill drew criticism from landlords who believe increases if financially indexed instead would prove less expensive over a three- to ten-year period (APPG-PRS, 2023). Tenants felt increases should be restricted to twice yearly (MHCLG, 2018).

Seventy-nine per cent of landlords surveyed were opposed to the abolition of Section 21 no-fault evictions and the proposed model for tenancy changes evoked concerns from landlords that they will no longer have 'control over their property' (MHCLG, 2018). The consensus amongst tenants and tenant support groups was in favour of discontinuing Section 21 (Crisis, 2023; HCCPA, 2022a, 2022b, 2022c). Generation Rent acknowledged that landlords need to be able to have lawful means at their disposal to recover their properties but at the same time, tenants should be able to live securely and have the right to raise complaints without fear of retaliatory eviction (APPG-PRS, 2023).

Tenants engage poorly with government surveys and consultations. The DLUHC are finding difficulty in targeting 'guidance and support schemes towards vulnerable tenants' owing to a limited understanding of their experiences, the underlying causes and their impacts (HCCPA, 2022d; MHCLG, 2018). Repeatedly asking tenants about alternative tenancy models elicits the response that they wanted better security of tenure and felt longer tenancies would provide more security and freedom to make long-term plans. Tenants were overwhelmingly in favour of a proposed three-year tenancy model, whereas landlords were not (MHCLG, 2018). The proposal detailed a six-month break clause allowing either party to end the tenancy with no penalty. Fifty-two per cent of landlords and 50% of tenants agreed that six months was a sufficient length. But many tenants were also concerned the clause could be open to abuse by landlords leaving them vulnerable to insecurity of tenure by routinely ending tenancies. Looking for somewhere else to live every six months made the proposal seem no different to a six-month AST with two months' notice. When asked again about fixed-term tenancies, 40% of tenants felt it should be for two years, whilst 65% of landlords wanted them for six months (DLUHC, 2022a).

The government hoped that by making periodic tenancies flexible, it would address tenants' concerns over inability to make long-term plans under short fixed-term tenancies that restrict their ability to move should their personal situations change. Similarly, for landlords, periodic tenancies they hoped would have provided more flexibility to gain possession when required (DLUHC, 2023a). But government surveys have found that tenants feel unable to negotiate their preferences with landlords over periodic or fixed-term tenancies and both parties find tenancy law to be complex (DLUHC, 2022a; MHCLG, 2018).

Many landlords surveyed whose relationship with their tenants is good, regard current systems as providing sufficient flexibility to extend tenancies. These landlords prefer a 6–12-month model and expressed concerns that longer tenancies could lead to property neglect. Up to 34% of landlords surveyed had offered tenancies over 12 months either on tenant's requests or because they felt this would provide a guaranteed income (MHCLG, 2018). When surveyed on longer tenancies again in 2019, 40% of landlords and agents were willing to offer tenancies longer than 12 months. A further 38% of landlords and agents indicated willingness to offer longer tenancies providing there was a mutual break clause. Seventy per cent of landlords and agents were agreeable to providing longer tenancies with mechanisms in place to allow easier eviction of difficult tenants (MHCLG, 2019).

The government believed the Private Renters Property Ombudsman that was to have been established under the Renters (Reform) Bill would settle landlord and tenant disputes without needing litigation thus ensuring landlords address tenants' complaints (DLUHC, 2022a). Enabling citizens to 'take control of their own lives' in this way would need a reformative structure placing the relationship between public services staff and service users at its heart (Quilter-Pinner and Khan, 2023).

Ninety-four per cent of landlords agreed they should be able to gain possession to use the property as a family home and 89% said there should be no qualifying requirement to evidence that a family member had previously resided at the property. Seventy-four per cent wanted a two-month notice period for these purposes, whilst 70% agreed that courts should be able to grant possession orders with proof of intention to sell the property (DLUHC, 2022a). This can only feasibly work if the court system becomes more efficient through improvements such as digitalisation.

Three years on from its inception, the evaluation of Rent Smart Wales found tenants' awareness of the scheme was poor (Griffiths, 2018). This is problematic because the Renters (Reform) Bill (2023) placed strong reliance upon tenants to use the ombudsman or report unlawful evictions either on grounds not set out in their tenancy agreements or because the three-month no-let period was abused and yet tenants have a poor understanding of their rights and often do not engage when canvassed for their views (MHCLG, 2018; Reeve-Lewis et al., 2022; Spencer et al., 2020). Generation Rent felt tenants would be more motivated to engage if they could be compensated for illegal eviction (APPG-PRS, 2023).

Downie (2018) and Tsai et al. (2020) call for better data on homelessness which has a weak evidence base. Historically, Section 21 evictions which do not require justification make it difficult to identify trends in homelessness statistics and reasons for eviction but the removal of Section 21 and the proposed amendments to the Housing Act 1988 under the Renters (Reform) Bill (2023) had potential to enable local authorities and government to improve data. Downie (2018) and Tsai et al. (2020) agree that better research could inform intervention and prevention methods making them more effective. Tsai et al. (2020) argue that illegal evictions, being locked out, deprived of services or having personal property removed need more research to better inform intervention and prevention methods. Agreement is found with Reeve-Lewis et al. (2022), because this data is not routinely collected, Safer Renting have now established an annual count of illegal evictions and harassment across England and Wales that can be routinely collected at a single point and measured as a 'benchmark figure'. Safer Renting has also established an annual count of the number of prosecutions carried out under the Protection from Eviction Act 1977 and the evidence of offences committed that breach the act across England and Wales. Safer Renting feels the most important reason to establish the record is because ignoring criminal behaviour trivialises illegal evictions and the severity of emotional and psychological harm caused to occupiers from the impact of being made homeless following a sustained 'campaign of intimidation'.

Tsai et al.'s (2020) study relied on tenants to self-report illegal eviction. Reeve-Lewis et al. (2022) do not see this as a valid measure for their purposes owing to tenants having a poor understanding of their rights. The measure used by Safer Renting is sourced from complaints reported and assessed by housing professionals for reliability and validity where the nature of the complaint constitutes an offence under the Protection from Eviction Act 1977. The data draws on different agency sources to create the single point of collection. Overtime, it is hoped that national scrutiny will strengthen the data through yearly analysis that identifies trends and trajectories ensuring the problem does not remain ignored. Centralised data on illegal eviction, harassment or persistent withdrawal of services could be accessed by officers and used as a 'replicable measure' to inform and reduce problems with inadequate homeless assessments (Reeve-Lewis et al., 2022). No matter how precise the count is, it will always underestimate the scale of the problem because ultimately it is reliant upon victims being 'willing and able to access' help (Spencer and Rugg, 2023).

Many retaliatory evictions do not correctly follow eviction procedures often unchallenged by tenants with little knowledge of their rights or how to exercise them (HCCPA, 2022a, 2022b, 2022c). Incorrect eviction procedures are often excused by the argument that landlords generally commit offences through ignorance and need more education from enforcers rather than regulation, because they cannot realistically be expected to update themselves on legislative changes to 'complex housing law'. This argument brushes over criminal landlords who offend knowingly or recklessly. It also discards the principle that criminal standards of proof and investigation are required to regulate and deter (Spencer et al., 2020).

The MOJ (2023) collate annual crime data including prosecutions under the Protection from Eviction Act 1977. During 2021, there were 112 prosecutions resulting in 29 convictions. In 2022, the number of prosecutions reduced to 48 of which 26 were convicted. Spencer and Rugg (2023) state that whilst there were fewer prosecutions brought about in 2022, the rate of conviction shows that these cases were better targeted even though the conviction rate is slightly lower than the previous year. Overall, these figures are not representative of the scale of the problem but rather illustrate the willingness or reluctance of local authorities to act. The Safer Renting illegal eviction count collated from their own data and that provided by Shelter, Citizens Advice, Legal Aid and H-Clic show that in 2021, there were 7,341 reported offences and 8,748 in 2022.

Data on increasing rates of eviction needs evaluation to determine which subgroups in society are most affected and to also understand the underlying causes to provide suitably adapted support services on a case-by-case basis to assist with debt management and resolve nuisance or anti-social behaviour (Van Laere et al., 2009).

In 2019 when landlords were asked about their plans for their portfolios over the next two years, 11% were planning to increase them whilst 53% of landlords surveyed were not intending any increases. Ten per cent of landlords whose portfolios represent 18% of tenancies in the sample surveyed indicated they wish to reduce their portfolios. Five per cent of landlords were proposing to sell their portfolio and leave the market representing 5% of tenancies (MHCLG, 2019). In 2021, a survey of 9,000 landlords with deposits registered under government schemes found 12% of landlords intended to decrease their portfolios and 10% of landlords intended selling off their portfolio, most commonly the reasons for this were attributed to recent legislation affecting tax relief, stamp duty and benefits. Over 11% of those wishing to downsize or sell off also stated that the inevitable abolition of Section 21 notices was a decisive factor. A smaller proportion said it was because of retirement or other reasons. Eleven per cent of landlords intended to increase their portfolio, whilst 48% intended to keep their portfolio the same size (DLUHC, 2022c).

In the 2019 survey, 46% of landlords said they bought property as an investment, 44% bought to enhance their pension with only 4% letting as a full-time business. Thirty-two per cent had originally intended to live in the properties, the majority of those surveyed having only recently become landlords, whilst 53% bought them directly to rent and 7% had inherited properties (MHCLG, 2019).

Ultimately acceptability of any reformation to the private rented sector through the abolition of section 21 and potential replacement amendments to the Housing Act 1988 will depend on whether the courts have undergone sufficient parallel reformatory processes (APPG-PRS, 2023; HCCPA, 2023; Quilter-Pinner and Khan, 2023), one cannot take place without the other and would be reliant upon AST's transition to periodic tenancies being facilitated through a phased approach whereby new tenancies will be periodic, and AST's will all transform to periodic after a 12-month interval (Cromarty, 2024). Amending section 8 whilst retaining section 21 on pause conceivably creates inequalities strengthening landlords' rights but leaving tenants vulnerable to no-fault removal and homelessness (Crisis, 2023), an unacceptable scenario for tenant support groups (HCCPA, 2022a, 2022b, 2022c) which will fail to deliver on the promised security of tenure. Conversely doing away with Section 21 evictions without putting the new measures in place for landlords to gain possession will not deliver on assurances that they will have control of their properties (DLUHC, 2023a; MHCLG, 2018). This would still leave courts exposed to the same problem of having to cope with a workload generated from this new legislation without sufficient reform. The property portal and associated enforcement measures and ombudsman schemes that were to be bought in with the now defunct Renters (Reform) Bill (2023) could be implemented but were largely designed to oversee regulation of new periodic tenancies and strongly reliant on the new tenancies being able to incorporate new grounds under the Housing Act 1988 and intended to replace a repealed section 21 (APPG-PRS, 2023; DLUHC, 2023a; HCCPA, 2023; Wilson and Cromarty, 2023).

Reformation of the private rented sector is strongly reliant upon legal and enforcement actors to be in place for the implementation to be feasible. But with further clarification regarding the roles and responsibilities of the different actors that have oversight of any new measures (LGA, 2023). The problem is made worse by the existing skills shortage in local government (LGA, 2022) and lessons from Rent Smart Wales whose legislative changes have taken a similar route should inform policymakers that local authority's capacity to proactively oversee such measures are only acceptable and feasible if there are sufficient resources in place to manage workloads (Griffiths, 2018; LGA, 2022). Any new attempt to resurrect a Renters (Reform) Bill would need provision of issue guidance on practices and procedures for local authorities to fully understand their roles and responsibilities.

References

ACORN. (2023, November). Written Evidence. House of Commons Public Bill Committee. Renters (Reform) Bill. RRB24.

APPG for the Private Rented Sector. (2023, December). *Ensuring Rental Reform Works for Tenants and Landlords. A Vision for the Private Rented Sector of the Future*. Propertymark. Available from: https://www.propertymark.co.uk/static/fe6fd918-c274-405f-813539a518191797/Ensuring-Rental-Reform-Works-for-Tenants-and-Landlords.pdf

Bolt Burdon Kemp LLP. (2023). *Inequality within Britain's Legal Aid Funding System*. [online]. Available from: https://www.bolt

burdonkemp.co.uk/our-insights/campaigns/inequality-in-britains-legal-aid-funding-system/

Bright, S. (2019). *Using Enforcement Powers to Move Occupiers Out.* Available from: https://www.law.ox.ac.uk/housing-after-grenfell/blog/2019/08/using-enforcement-powers-move-occupiers-out

Burns, A. and Hadfield, T. (2018, November). *A Qualitative Research Investigation of the Factors Influencing the Progress, Timescales and Outcomes of Housing Cases in County Courts.* London: Ministry of Housing, Communities and Local Government.

Chartered Institute of Environmental Health (CIEH). (2023, November). Written Evidence. House of Commons Public Bill Committee. Renters (Reform) Bill. RRB50.

Citizens Advice. (2023, June 15). 'An End to Unfair Evictions?', *citizensadvice.org.uk.* [online]. Available from: https://www.citizensadvice.org.uk/about-us/our-work/policy/policy-research-topics/housing-policy-research/an-end-to-unfair-evictions/

Citizens Advice Newcastle and Gatesehead. (2023, November). Written Evidence. House of Commons Public Bill Committee. Renters (Reform) Bill. RRB41.

Crisis. (2023, November). Written Evidence. House of Commons Public Bill Committee. Renters (Reform) Bill. RRB21.

Cromarty, H. (2024). Renters (Reform) Bill 2023–24: Progress of the Bill. *House of Commons library.* (18 April 2024). No. 10004. London.

Department for Communities and Local Government. (2017, March). *English Housing Survey Headline Report 2015–16.* London: DCLG.

Department for Levelling Up, Housing and Communities. (2022a, May 11). *Government to Deliver 'New Deal' for Renters.* London: DLUHC.

Department for Levelling Up, Housing and Communities. (2022b, December). *English Housing Survey Headline Report 2021–22.* London: DLUHC.

Department for Levelling Up, Housing and Communities. (2022c, May 26). *English Private Landlord Survey 2021.* London: DLUHC.

Department for Levelling Up, Housing and Communities. (2023a, May 12). *Renters (Reform) Bill Impact Assessment: DLUHC 2564.* London: DLUHC.

Department for Levelling Up, Housing and Communities. (2023b, May 17). *Guide to the Renters (Reform) Bill.* London: DLUHC.

Deregulation Act 2015 c.20. Available from: https://www.legislation.gov.uk/ukpga/2015/20/contents/enacted

Dhesi, S. (2019). *Tackling Health Inequalities: Reinventing the Role of Environmental Health.* First Edition. London: Routledge.

Doran, K., Guzzardo, J., Hill, K., Kitterlin, N., Li, W. and Liebl, R. (2003). *No Time for Justice: A Study of Chicago's Eviction Court.* Illinois: Lawyers' Committee for Better Housing, Chicago-Kent School of Law, Illinois Institute of Technology.

Downie, M. ed. (2018). 'Everybody in: How to End Homelessness in Great Britain', *Crisis*. [online]. Available from: https://www.crisis. org.uk/media/239951/everybody_in_how_to_end_homelessness_ in_great_britain_2018.pdf

Gold, A.E. (2016). 'No Home for Justice: How Eviction Perpetuates Health Inequity Among Low-Income and Minority Tenants', *Georgetown Journal on Poverty Law and Policy*, 24(1), pp. 59–88.

Griffiths, L. (2018, June 30). *Evaluation of Rent Smart Wales Implementation and Delivery.* Cardiff: Welsh Government.

Hartman, C. and Robinson, D. (2003). 'Evictions: The Hidden Housing Problem', *Housing Policy Debate*. [online]. Available from: https://doi.org/10.1080/10511482.2003.9521483

Hoke, M.K. and Boen, C.E. (2021) 'The Health Impacts of Eviction: Evidence from the National Longitudinal Study of Adolescent to Adult Health', *Social Science & Medicine (1982)*, 273, p. 113742.

House of Commons Committee of Public Accounts. (2022a, January). Written Evidence Submitted by ACORN. PRP0003.

House of Commons Committee of Public Accounts. (2022b, January). Written Evidence Submitted by StepChange Debt Charity. PRP0005.

House of Commons Committee of Public Accounts. (2022c, January). Written Evidence Submitted by Glass Door Homeless Charity. PRP0006.

House of Commons Committee of Public Accounts. (2022d, January). Written Evidence Submitted by Transparency International UK. PRP0007.

House of Commons Committee of Public Accounts. (2023, June 30). *Progress on the Courts and Tribunals Reform Programme: HC 1002.* London: House of Commons.

House of Commons Work and Pensions Committee. (2014, March 26). *Support for Housing Costs in the Reformed Welfare System. Fourth Report of Session 2013–14: HC 720.* London: House of Commons.

Housing Act 1988 c.50. *legislation.gov.uk.* [online]. Available from: https://www.legislation.gov.uk/ukpga/1988/50/contents

Housing Act 2004 c.34. *legislation.gov.uk.* [online]. Available from: https://www.legislation.gov.uk/ukpga/2004/34/contents

Land Compensation Act 1973 c.26. Available from: https://www.legislation.gov.uk/ukpga/1973/26/contents

The Law Society. (2022, October). *Solicitors' Views on the Court Infrastructure. Are the Physical Buildings and Technology Fit for*

Purpose? Available from: https://www.lawsociety.org.uk/topics/research/are-our-courts-fit-for-purpose

Local Government Association. (2022, May). *Local Government Workforce Survey 2022, Research Report*. London: LGA.

Local Government Association. (2023, November 7). 'Renters' Reform Bill, Committee Stage, House of Commons', *local.gov.uk*. Available from: https://www.local.gov.uk/parliament/briefings-and-responses/renters-reform-bill-committee-stage-house-commons-7-november

Lonegrass, M.T. (2015). 'Eliminating Landlord Retaliation in England and Wales – Lessons from the United States', *Louisiana Law Review*, 75(4), pp. 1071–1123.

Makinson, R. (2021, August 26). 'LASPO: How A Near-Decade of Legal Aid Cuts Has Affected Britain's Most Vulnerable', *Lawyer Monthly*. [online]. Available from: https://www.lawyer-monthly.com/2021/08/laspo-how-a-near-decade-of-legal-aid-cuts-has-affected-britains-most-vulnerable/

Ministry of Housing, Communities & Local Government. (2018, January 25). *English Housing Survey 2016 to 2017: headline report*. MHCLG. London.

Ministry of Housing Communities and Local Government. (2019, January). *English Private Landlord Survey 2018*. London: MHCLG.

Ministry of Justice. (2023, February 9). 'Mortgage and Landlord Possession Statistics: October to December 2022', *Gov.UK*. [online]. Available from: https://www.gov.uk/government/statistics/mortgage-and-landlord-possession-statistics-october-to-december-2022

Moffatt, R. (2022). 'Developing Effective PRS Regulatory Strategies', in Stewart, J. and Moffatt, R. (Eds), *Regulating the Privately Rented Housing Sector*. Abingdon, Oxon: Routledge, pp. 115–122. Available from: https://doi.org/10.1201/9781003246534-14

Morestin, F. (2012, September). *A Framework for Analyzing Public Policies: Practical Guide*. National Collaborating Centre for Healthy Public Policy. [online]. Available from: http://www.ncchpp.ca/docs/Guide_framework_analyzing_policies_En.pdf

National Audit Office. (2021, December 10). *Regulation of Private Renting: HC 863*. London: Department for Levelling Up, Housing & Communities.

Oatt, P. (2019). *Selective Licensing: The Basis for a Collaborative Approach to Addressing Health Inequalities*. Abingdon. Oxon: Routledge.

Office of the Deputy Prime Minister. (2006, February). *Housing Health and Safety Rating System Enforcement Guidance*. London: ODPM.

Peaker, G. (2023, May 17). 'Renters (Reform) Bill – the Good, the Potentially Good and the Ugly. Part 1', *Nearly Legal*. [online].

Available from: https://nearlylegal.co.uk/2023/05/renters-reform-bill-the-good-the-potentially-good-and-the-ugly-part-1/

Propertymark. (2023, November). Written Evidence. House of Commons Public Bill Committee. Renters (Reform) Bill. RRB48.

Protection from Eviction Act 1977 c.43. Available from: https://www.legislation.gov.uk/ukpga/1977/43

Quilter-Pinner, H. and Khan, H. (2023, December). *Great Government Public Service Reform in the 2020s*. London: Institute for Public Policy Research.

Reeve-Lewis, B., Bolton, J.L. and Rugg, J. (2022, May). *Offences Under the Protection from Eviction Act 1977 in England and Wales: A Report from Safer Renting*. London: Safer Renting. Cambridge House.

Renters (Reform) Bill. (2023, December 7). Department for Levelling Up, Housing and Communities. House of Commons.

Residential Landlord's Association. (2016, February 22). Written Evidence Submitted by the Residential Landlord's Association [HOL 111].

Residential Landlord's Association. (2017, September). Written Evidence Submitted by the Residential Landlord's Association [UCR 0028].

Richards, G. and Davies, N. (2023, October 30). *Performance Tracker 2023: Criminal Courts*. Institute for Government. Available from: https://www.instituteforgovernment.org.uk/publication/performance-tracker-2023/criminal-courts

Sagoe, C., Ehrlich, R., Reynolds, L. and Rich, H. (2020). *Time for Change: Marking Renting Fairer for Private Landlords*. London: Shelter.

Simcock, T.J. (2018). *Investigating the Effect of Welfare Reform on Private Renting*. Manchester, UK: Residential Landlords Association.

Smith, D. (2023, May 17). *Renters' Reform Finally Arrives*. JMW Solicitors LLP. [online]. Available from: https://www.jmw.co.uk/blog/commercial-litigation-dispute-resolution/renters-reform-finally-arrives

Spencer, R., Reeve-Lewis, B., Rugg, J. and Barata, E. (2020). *Journeys in the Shadow Private Rented Sector*. London: Cambridge House/Centre for Housing Policy, p. 47.

Spencer, R. and Rugg, J. (2023, November). *Offences Under the Protection from Eviction Act 1977 in England- 2022 Update of the Annual Count, Safer Renting*. Available from: https://ch1889.org/wp-content/uploads/2023/12/PfEA-2022-offences-count-Safer-Renting-11-2023.pdf

Steinberg, J.K. (2015, February). 'Demand Side Reform in the Poor People's Court', *Connecticut Law Review*, 47(3), pp. 741–808.

Steiner v Liverpool City Council. (2019). MAN/OOBY/HPO/2019/0004.

Tsai, J., Jones, N., Szymkowiak, D. and Rosenheck, R.A. (2020). 'Longitudinal Study of the Housing and Mental Health Outcomes of Tenants Appearing in Eviction Court', *Social Psychiatry and Psychiatric Epidemiology*, 56(9), pp. 1679–1686.

Tucker, H. (2023, June 9). *The Renters' Reform Bill: Changes to Grounds for Possession. Local Government Lawyer*. [online]. Available from: https://www.localgovernmentlawyer.co.uk/housing-law/315-housing-features/54092-the-renters-reform-bill-changes-to-grounds-for-possession

Tunstall, H., Pickett, K. and Johnsen, S. (2010). 'Residential Mobility in the UK During Pregnancy and Infancy: Are Pregnant Women, New Mothers and Infants 'Unhealthy Migrants'?', *Social Science and Medicine*, 71(4), pp. 786–798.

UK Parliament. (2023). *The Future of Legal Aid*. House of Commons. [online]. Available from: https://committees.parliament.uk/work/531/the-future-of-legal-aid/

Van Laere, I., De Wit, M. and Klazinga, N. (2009) 'Evaluation of the Signalling and Referral System for Households at Risk of Eviction in Amsterdam', *Health & Social Care in the Community*, 17(1), pp. 1–8. Available from: https://doi.org/10.1111/j.1365-2524.2007.00790.x (accepted 20 March 2008).

Wilson, W. (2023, October 30). *Can Private Landlords Refuse to Let to Benefit Claimants and People with Children?* London: House of Commons Library.

Wilson, W. and Cromarty, H. (2018, December 14). *The Homes (Fitness for Human Habitation) Bill 2017–19. CBP 08195*. London: House of Commons Library.

Wilson, W. and Cromarty, H. (2023, October 21). *Research Briefing: Renters (Reform) Bill 2022–23: CBP08756*. London: House of Commons Library.

Zewde, N., Eliason, E., Allen, H. and Gross, T. (2019). 'The Effects of the ACA Medicaid Expansion on Nationwide Home Evictions and Eviction-Court Initiations: United States, 2000–2016', *American Journal of Public Health (1971)*, 109(10), pp. 1379–1383.

8 Reforming the Private Rented Sector

Housing policy has been adversely shaped by market forces where lack of affordable rental homes of good quality are unable to meet housing demand (Emmerson et al., 2020). The growth of the private rented sector has stagnated, increasing rents and frozen housing allowances paid in arrears are making this an unaffordable choice for households, exacerbated by policy capture and price setting within a poorly regulated sector.

The intentions of the Housing Act 1988 to provide security of tenure were undermined from the start with the sanctioning of retaliatory evictions under Section 21. When compared to the American court systems for eviction, for all their faults retaliatory, eviction is not seen as legitimate. Ending Section 21 evictions is a welcome policy enactment that will contribute to reducing stress through the insecurity of tenure along with restrictions on rental increases, but this alone is insufficient without improved policies to address housing conditions (Clair et al., 2023).

The Renters (Reform) Bill (2023) is dead, but had it continued, it was highly unlikely that all elements could have been enabled without sufficient court reformation (APPG-PRS, 2023; HCCPA, 2023, Quilter-Pinner and Khan, 2023). Had an enactment of the bill bought in periodic tenancies on a set date, it follows that ASTs still currently issued would overlap with this implementation. A two-tier system would be in place whereby Section 21 no-fault evictions would still be applicable to existing ASTs whilst any new tenancies created would have to be periodic (Cromarty, 2024). This would most likely cause confusion and be difficult for enforcing authorities and courts under reformation to accommodate. Eventually, existing ASTs would expire and become periodic, effectively killing off Section 21 evictions. Upon the expiry of an AST, a landlord would not lawfully be able to rely upon any of the new eviction grounds unless they enter new

DOI: 10.1201/9781032705071-8

periodic tenancy agreements with their tenants wherein those clauses are included. Landlords would have risked being fined for unlawful evictions that rely upon grounds they have omitted from these periodic tenancies. This will be strongly reliant upon tenants to be aware of their rights for local authorities to be vigilant and crucially, for landlords to understand these new requirements.

The unexpected calling of a parliamentary election dissolved parliament leaving the Renters (Reform) Bill unfinished (Cobbold, 2024). A new government may yet take up the reins but historically successive governments creating laws and guidance for use by local authorities have ideological differences in how to oversee policy. Reformation of public services is often outlined from the perspective of seemingly polarised views arguing for more investment and growth of the state or reformative measures to shrink the state particularly healthcare and legal sectors (Quilter-Pinner and Khan, 2023). Labour governments advocate improving health and addressing inequalities at the population level whilst Conservative governments rely upon a 'trickle down' effect through economic recovery (Dhesi, 2019). As seen in the costs chapter, market stagnation negates effects that would otherwise see investment and economic growth produce an income that trickles down through society. Theoretically, this unequally distributed income provides sufficient economic gain for redistributed funding of public goods that otherwise would be unavailable along with progressive taxes, allowing more financial retention at lower income levels. The effect is reduced when societal inequalities widen despite what official income data shows because these figures do not reflect reductions in public services and goods, inequalities in purchasing power and the housing markets' inelasticity of supply (Friedman, 2006; Greenwood and Holt, 2010).

Quilter-Pinner and Khan (2023) believe the polarised narratives of growth or shrinkage are a distraction and what is required is a smarter state using a combined approach. Dhesi (2019) notes right-leaning governments are less likely to commit to long-term monitoring of inequalities compared to left-leaning governments who would do so irrespective of whether the results were favourable or not.

The sustainability of tenure needs short-term financial support to prevent arrears and eviction. This is a durable strategy that will enable low-income households to overcome the insecurity of tenure and reduce associated increasing health burdens enabling households to budget effectively, set down roots and allow children to have better educational opportunities (Acharya et al., 2022; Coley et al., 2013; Moran-McCabe et al., 2018). The policy of freezing allowance rates or setting them at a 30th percentile level without taking into account the rate of rental increases across broad market areas will only provide a durable measure of relief in the short term (Emmerson et al., 2020; Wilson, 2023) and only for those tenants able to be accommodated in affordable local properties of which policies will have to be made to ensure there is an increased supply for this all to work (Acharya et al., 2022; Moran-McCabe et al., 2018) along with robust and proactive housing enforcement measures to reduce hazards to health (Coley et al., 2013). This requires policies with cross-party consensus to be embedded that extend beyond the five-year cycle of an election period with equitable input from all stakeholders.

Living in adequate accommodation without fear of eviction is a right that should be incorporated into policy underpinning housing strategies (OHCHR, 2009). It is essential that public health advocates emphasise the need for policymakers to adhere to human rights legislation within housing policy and strategies ensuring their full implementation and enforcement (Thiele, 2002). Failure to evaluate these legislative effects promptly leaves the public exposed to interventions that fail to deliver promised protections doing more harm than good (Moran-McCabe et al., 2018).

Being unable to afford rent is a primary catalyst for lawful or unlawful evictions and behind this are the causal factors of poverty that increase the likelihood of forced removal and its related health effects. The focus of the prevention of eviction should be considered an 'essential public health promotion' (Acharya et al., 2022). To this end, housing policy should shift focus from commercialisation, investment and owner occupancy to primarily being health-based. This would not prevent housing from being prosperous as a derived benefit of a health-based policy, whereas the reverse has not been found to be true of commercialisation (Thiele, 2002).

The effects of eviction upon tenants' mental health can linger for up to eight years after the event and these effects are more profound than any inconvenience imposed through forced relocation (Hatch and Yun, 2021). The overall downward trend in social housing evictions is encouraging and will have a positive impact on public health. But a concern remains about the steady increase of private rented sector evictions (MOJ, 2023). Overall global data shows a strong association with poor health outcomes for mothers whose children are disadvantaged across the social gradient. Policy makers should consider whether security of tenure brought about through policy reformation will provide sufficient preventative health care measures not only in terms of reducing Category 1 hazards of damp and mould or excess cold and making savings on health care treatment but also to see what effect the policy has on associations with homelessness, stress, child development and related illnesses (DLUHC, 2022, 2023; Hatch and Yun, 2021; Hazekamp et al., 2020; Marmot, 2020; NAO, 2021).

In areas where the prevalence of eviction increases whether legal or illegal, more must be done to use data to learn what the specific causal factors are and adapt services to address lawful and illegal evictions, debt management, anti-social behaviour or provide a gateway to social care (MOJ, 2023; Reeve-Lewis et al., 2022; Van Laere et al., 2009). In this respect, the Renters (Reform) Bill's database and the property portal would have been valuable resources with scope to use the data in conjunction with EHS and public health data. Access to such resources should also be allowed for academic researchers to help create and develop more evidence-based policy (CIEH, 2023).

Whosoever is in power following the election, a new government will have to devise policy to support householders on low incomes whose security of tenure is at risk during the economic downturn. In 2019, security of tenure was being considered through a proposed two-year agreement before most eviction grounds could be used (MHCLG, 2019). This proposal was welcomed by tenant support organisations who made their preferences clear during consultation (ACORN, 2023; Citizens Advice Newcastle and Gateshead, 2023; Shelter, 2023). Periodic tenancies potentially heighten the risk of eviction every six months (Propertymark, 2023). The government is aware through their own research that most tenants do not understand their rights (MHCLG, 2018; NAO, 2021) and in order to be able to challenge rental increases, there must be an information and awareness campaign to promote such legislative changes and allow tenants and landlords to understand those rights and expectations, reducing abuse and non-compliance of the system as well as the civil and criminal burdens on courts and tribunals (LGA, 2023).

The resources and skills required amongst regulating authorities are lacking and the changes proposed under the now defunct Renters (Reform) Bill raise questions about their feasibility and whether the resources amongst housing regulators will be capable of delivering successful implementation (LGA, 2022, 2023). There is clearly a role for technology and machine learning to facilitate local authority statutory functions (Moffatt, 2022). Had things progressed albeit with Section 21 abolition indefinitely paused, the introduction of more enforcement tools and legislation to protect tenants from eviction would be insufficient to address widespread problems within the housing system because intervention is required on numerous levels requiring tailoring to the particular needs and wants of different communities where drivers of affordability are directly related to the characteristics of local economies (Moran-McCabe et al., 2018; Quigley and Raphael, 2004). Local authorities place reliance upon suitably allocated investment to support gradual transitions to models of self-funding enforcement (CIEH, 2023; Propertymark, 2023).

The Renters (Reform) Bill (2023) was an opportunity to redress the balance between landlords and tenants but lessons from its evaluation show that another piece of legislation on its own will be insufficient without resourcing enforcement and legal services. Any future housing policy reformations should not be unnecessarily delayed by ongoing court reformations. Serious consideration should be given to expedient investment in a new housing court with the provision of more funding to legal aid to accommodate the anticipated workload. Funding streams should be made available for local authorities to resource housing enforcement, and there should be more equitability amongst stakeholders on future housing policy consultations.

Finally, just as a constant churn of tenancies creates housing market instabilities so too does a churn of revolving door leadership at ministerial level. Tenancy reform needs not only greater security of tenure but also consistency and durability in leadership at the ministerial level.

References

Acharya, B., Bhatta, D. and Dhakal, C. (2022). 'The Risk of Eviction and the Mental Health Outcomes Among the US Adults', *Preventive Medicine Reports*, 29, pp. 101981–101981. Available from: https://doi.org/10.1016/j.pmedr.2022.101981

ACORN. (2023, October). *Renters Manifesto Policy Document*. Available at; https://www.rentermanifesto.org/read_the_manifesto_full

APPG for the Private Rented Sector. (2023, December). *Ensuring Rental Reform Works for Tenants and Landlords. A Vision for the Private Rented Sector of the Future*. Propertymark. Available from: https://www.

propertymark.co.uk/static/fe6fd918-c274-405f-813539a518191797/Ensuring-Rental-Reform-Works-for-Tenants-and-Landlords.pdf

Chartered Institute of Environmental Health (CIEH). (2023, November). Written Evidence. House of Commons Public Bill Committee. Renters (Reform) Bill. RRB50.

Citizens Advice Newcastle and Gateshead. (2023, November 23). Written evidence submitted by Citizens Advice Newcastle and Citizens Advice Gateshead Joint Submission to the Renters Reform Bill Committee for Parliamentary Scrutiny (RRB41). Available at; https://www.parallelparliament.co.uk/bills/2022-23/rentersreform

Clair, A., Baker, E. and Kumari, M. (2023). 'Are Housing Circumstances Associated with Faster Epigenetic Ageing?', *Journal of Epidemiology and Community Health*. Published Online First: 10 October 2023. Available from: https://doi.org/10.1136/jech-2023-220523

Cobbold, N. (2024 May 31). Renters (Reform) Bill dead. Reapit. Available at; https://www.reapit.com/content-hub/renters-reform-bill-dead

Coley, R.L., Leventhal, T., Lynch, A.D. and Kull, M. (2013, September). *Poor Quality Housing is Tied to Children's Emotional and Behavioral Problems. Policy Research Brief.* Chicago: MacArthur Foundation.

Cromarty, H. (2024). Renters (Reform) Bill 2023–24: Progress of the Bill. *House of Commons library*. (18 April 2024). No. 10004. London.

Department for Levelling Up, Housing and Communities. (2022, May 26). *English Private Landlord Survey 2021*. London: DLUHC.

Department for Levelling Up, Housing and Communities. (2023, May 12). *Renters (Reform) Bill Impact Assessment: DLUHC 2564*. London: DLUHC.

Dhesi, S. (2019). *Tackling Health Inequalities: Reinventing the Role of Environmental Health*. First Edition. London: Routledge.

Emmerson, C., Johnson, P., Stockton, I., Waters, T. and Zaranko, B. (2020, November 25). *Initial Reaction from IFS Researchers on Spending Review 2020 and OBR Forecasts*. Institute for Fiscal Studies. [online]. Available from: https://ifs.org.uk/news/initial-reaction-ifs-researchers-spending-review-2020-and-obr-forecasts

Friedman, B. (2006). 'The Moral Consequences of Economic Growth', *Society (New Brunswick)*, 43(2), pp. 15–22.

Greenwood, D.T. and Holt, R.P.F. (2010). 'Growth, Inequality and Negative Trickle Down', *Journal of Economic Issues*, 44(2), pp. 403–410.

Hatch, M.E. and Yun, J. (2021) 'Losing Your Home is Bad for Your Health: Short- and Medium-Term Health Effects of Eviction on

Young Adults', *Housing Policy Debate*, 31(3–5), pp. 469–489. Available from: https://doi.org/10.1080/10511482.2020.1812690

Hazekamp, C., Yousuf, S., Day, K., Daly, M.K. and Sheehan, K. (2020) 'Eviction and Pediatric Health Outcomes in Chicago', *Journal of Community Health*, 45(5), pp. 891–899. Available from: https://doi.org/10.1007/s10900-020-00806-y

House of Commons Committee of Public Accounts. (2023, June 30). *Progress on the Courts and Tribunals Reform Programme: HC 1002*. London: House of Commons.

Local Government Association. (2022, May). *Local Government Workforce Survey 2022, Research Report*. London: LGA.

Local Government Association. (2023, November 7). 'Renters' Reform Bill, Committee Stage, House of Commons', *local.gov.uk*. Available from: https://www.local.gov.uk/parliament/briefings-and-responses/renters-reform-bill-committee-stage-house-commons-7-november

Marmot, M. (2020, February 25). 'Health Equity in England: The Marmot Review 10 Years On', *BMJ*, 368.

Ministry of Housing Communities and Local Government. (2018). *Overcoming the Barriers to Longer Tenancies in the Private Rented Sector*. London: MHCLG. (updated 15 April 2019).

Ministry of Justice. (2023, February 9). 'Mortgage and Landlord Possession Statistics: October to December 2022', *Gov.UK*. [online]. Available from: https://www.gov.uk/government/statistics/mortgage-and-landlord-possession-statistics-october-to-december-2022

Moffatt, R. (2022). 'Developing Effective PRS Regulatory Strategies', in Stewart, J. and Moffatt, R. (Eds), *Regulating the Privately Rented Housing Sector*. Abingdon, Oxon: Routledge, pp. 115–122. Available from: https://doi.org/10.1201/9781003246534-14

Moran-McCabe, K., Gutman, A. and Burris, S. (2018) 'Public Health Implications of Housing Laws: Nuisance Evictions', *Public Health Reports (1974)*, 133(5), pp. 606–609. Available from: https://doi.org/10.1177/0033354918786725

National Audit Office. (2021, December 10). *Regulation of Private Renting: HC 863*. London: Department for Levelling Up, Housing & Communities.

OHCHR, U. (2009). *The Right to Adequate Housing*. Geneva, Switzerland: UN Office of the High Commissioner for Human Rights.

Propertymark. (2023, November). Written Evidence. House of Commons Public Bill Committee. Renters (Reform) Bill. RRB48.

Quigley, J.M. and Raphael, S. (2004). 'Is Housing Unaffordable? Why Isn't It More Affordable?', *The Journal of Economic Perspectives*, 18(1), pp. 191–214.

Quilter-Pinner, H. and Khan, H. (2023, December). *Great Government Public Service Reform in the 2020s*. London: Institute for Public Policy Research.

Reeve-Lewis, B., Bolton, J.L. and Rugg, J. (2022, May). *Offences Under the Protection from Eviction Act 1977 in England and Wales: A Report from Safer Renting*. London: Safer Renting. Cambridge House.

Renters (Reform) Bill. (2023, December 7). Department for Levelling Up, Housing and Communities. House of Commons.

Shelter (2023, November 14). Written evidence submitted by Shelter. Renters Reform Bill Committee for Parliamentary Scrutiny. (RRB09). Available at; https://www.parallelparliament. co.uk/bills/2022-23/rentersreform

Thiele, B. (2002). 'The Human Right to Adequate Housing: A Tool for Promoting and Protecting Individual and Community Health', *American Journal of Public Health*, 92(5), pp. 712–715.

Van Laere, I., De Wit, M. and Klazinga, N. (2009) 'Evaluation of the Signalling and Referral System for Households at Risk of Eviction in Amsterdam', *Health & Social Care in the Community*, 17(1), pp. 1–8. Available from: https://doi.org/10.1111/j.1365-2524.2007. 00790.x (accepted 20 March 2008).

Wilson, W. (2023, October 30). *Can Private Landlords Refuse to Let to Benefit Claimants and People with Children?* London: House of Commons Library.

Index

Note: Page numbers in *italics* indicate figures; page numbers in **bold** indicate tables.

For Product Safety Concerns and Information please contact our EU
representative GPSR@taylorandfrancis.com
Taylor & Francis Verlag GmbH, Kaufingerstraße 24, 80331 München, Germany

* 9 7 8 1 0 3 2 7 0 5 0 5 7 *